DEN OF MISERY

DEN OF MISERY

INDIANA'S CIVIL WAR PRISON

JAMES R. HALL

PELICAN PUBLISHING COMPANY
GRETNA 2006

The word "Pelican" and the depiction of a pelican are trademarks
of Pelican Publishing Company, Inc., and are registered in the
U.S. Patent and Trademark Office.

Library of Congress Cataloging-in-Publication Data

Hall, James R.
    Den of misery : Indiana's Civil War prison / James R. Hall.
        p. cm.
    Includes bibliographical references and index.
    ISBN-13: 978-1-58980-351-0 (hardcover : alk. paper)
    1. Camp Morton (Ind.) 2. Indianapolis (Ind.)—History—Civil
War, 1861-1865—Prisoners and prisons. 3. United States—
History—Civil War, 1861-1865—Prisoners and prisons. I. Title.
    E616.M8H35 2006
    973.7'72—dc22

                                                    2005036388

Printed in the United States of America
Published by Pelican Publishing Company, Inc.
1000 Burmaster Street, Gretna, Louisiana 70053

This book is dedicated to all of the young Civil War soldiers who lost their lives far from home and hearth in Northern and Southern military prisons.

It is also dedicated to my teachers at Pearson Elementary School in Shelbyville, Indiana, who helped to stimulate my interest in the American Civil War during centennial observances in the early and mid-1960s.

Finally, it is dedicated to my wife and best friend, Mary, who has somehow managed to put up with me all these years, a feat that certainly deserves special recognition (if not a medal).

Contents

Acknowledgments 9

Introduction 11

Chapter 1 "Shots" Are Fired on Camp Morton 17

Chapter 2 Under the Shade of Walnuts and Oaks 27

Chapter 3 Early Days of the Prison 35

Chapter 4 Darkness Falls on Camp Morton 41

Chapter 5 The Tightrope Walk at Camp Morton 49

Chapter 6 "Cold Cheer" and Coldhearted Murder 57

Chapter 7 A Stunned City and State React 65

Chapter 8 "Walking Skeletons" and Missing Food 73

Chapter 9 "A Demon in Human Flesh" 79

Chapter 10 Camp Morton's Final Days 91

Chapter 11 The Legacy of Camp Morton 101

Appendix 107

Notes 149

Bibliography 155

Index 157

Acknowledgments

I want to thank Pelican Publishing Company for its commitment to helping me to tell the stories of the young soldiers who lived and tragically died in Indiana's Camp Morton Civil War prison.

I want to thank the Indiana Historical Society and its fine staff for assisting me with this project in many ways.

Thanks to the library staff at the University of North Carolina at Chapel Hill for helping me with some photos used in this book.

I am also grateful to the staff at the Shelbyville-Shelby County Public Library in Shelbyville, Indiana, for helping me to obtain information through interlibrary loans.

I want to thank my friend Jeff Lahr for his computer-related counsel.

Because I can't drive due to vision disability, I want to thank my wife, Mary, for serving as my taxi driver for all of the auto excursions that were necessary in the preparation of this book.

I also want to thank two of my former newspaper editors, Al Horton and Jim McKinney. When I was a young reporter, Al taught me how to dig to get to the heart of a good story and Jim taught me how to tell a good story.

I want to thank my late dad, Russell Hall, for sparking my interest in Civil War history when he took me to Gettysburg the summer before I entered third grade.

Last, but certainly not least, I want to thank the Lord God, from whom all good gifts and all blessings flow.

Introduction

"(Wyeth) made clear for the first time how conditions in northern compounds, particularly at Morton and Elmira, were as inhuman as those at Andersonville."

When I was a young boy growing up in central Indiana during the 1960s and 1970s, I was taught a version of American history that was a mixture of fact and mythology. In those days (and to a somewhat lesser extent now), children were taught a sanitized version of U.S. history that ignored unsavory elements from America's past and often bordered on blatant nationalistic propaganda.

Back in the late 1950s, we were taught, for example, that George Armstrong Custer and other American "Indian fighters" were courageous men embracing a high calling of ridding the West of murderous barbarians.

The truth, as I later learned, was of course much different than what I was taught in public school back then. The atrocities America and Americans committed against Native Americans in stealing their land and sending them to "reservations" stand as a shameful blot on America's historic legacy as a moral and ethical nation.

When I began my career as a professional journalist in the 1970s, I determined to "tell the truth" about America and Americans, even if the truth would be considered objectionable to some people who prefer a sanitized and mythological version of history.

During my Indiana public-school days, I had been taught in state history classes about a Civil War prison in Indianapolis, Camp Morton. This Union prison, located in what is now a part of the inner city of one of America's largest cities, was considered during its time to be among the best of the Northern prison camps.

11

Hoosier public officials and military leaders boasted that prisoners were treated well at Camp Morton and that they were kept comfortable and safe by military personnel assigned to the prison with help from the general citizenry of Indianapolis.

Compared to legendary Civil War-era prisoner camps in the South (such as Andersonville) known for their cruelties and inhumane treatment of prisoners, Camp Morton has been represented in many contemporary, and some historical, accounts as a shining model of Christian virtue and humanism in the Indiana hinterlands.

But the real truth about Camp Morton is that it was a place of pain, suffering, brutality, and even murder. Far from its image as a kind of Waldorf-Astoria among Civil War prisons, Camp Morton was a place where young Southern soldiers struggled to survive with little protection against brutally cold winter weather and searing summer heat. It was a place where young men were often beaten, tortured, shot, and denied proper nutrition and medical treatment.

All of this was first brought to the attention of the nation a quarter-century after the end of the Civil War by a prominent physician and medical researcher, Dr. John A. Wyeth. A prisoner in Camp Morton during the war, Wyeth recounted the reprehensible conditions in the prison in an article in the April 1891 issue of *Century Monthly Magazine*.

Dr. Wyeth was responding to a Union propaganda campaign following the Civil War that decried dire conditions of Confederate prisons while ignoring those of its own.

"(Wyeth) made clear for the first time how conditions in northern compounds, particularly at Morton and Elmira, were as inhuman as those at Andersonville," wrote historian Bradley Omanson.[1]

Official estimates vary on how many Confederates died at Camp Morton, but some historians believe that close to two thousand prisoners never returned to their Southern homes, hearths, and loved ones.

Over time, the cruel legacy of Civil War prisons on both sides has been revealed and now the true historic legacy of Indiana's Camp Morton will be revealed in the pages of this book.

America's healing process from the Civil War continues with every passing generation. A full understanding of those times and the benchmark of suffering set during the Civil War continues to shape our national perspective on modern-day conflicts and events.

The truth about one of the North's most prominent Civil War-era prisons was a hot issue over one hundred years ago and it may still be a hot issue for some who prefer a sanitized and mythological view of American history. But while there is little, if anything, to be learned from pseudo-historic legend, much can be gained from understanding the truth.

It is to that end that I make every effort to present a true and accurate portrait of the sufferings and travails of multiple thousands of young Southern soldiers who lived—and who so often tragically died—at Indiana's Camp Morton during the turbulent years of the American Civil War.

I hope and expect that this book will reopen the Camp Morton controversy to further historical reflection, discussion, and debate.

Somewhere, the old Rebel from Alabama, Dr. Wyeth, must be smiling.

DEN OF MISERY

John A. Wyeth is shown here late in his life in a photo taken in 1914. Photo from Documenting the American South (http://docsouth.unc.edu), The University of North Carolina at Chapel Hill Libraries.

CHAPTER 1

"Shots" Are Fired on Camp Morton

More than a quarter of a century after the last Civil War salvo had been fired, Dr. John A. Wyeth, arguably the most famous American physician and medical researcher of his era, dropped a veritable bombshell on the entire state of Indiana and raised eyebrows throughout the nation with his startling article in the April 1891 issue of *Century Monthly Magazine.*

The article created a furor, resulting in letters in magazines and newspapers all across the North. Had he lived 100 years later, Wyeth would have no doubt been a popular guest on CNN, PBS, the Fox Network, and other network television news programs.

Wyeth, who had been a youthful soldier with the Fourth Alabama Cavalry during the American Civil War, had been a prisoner at Camp Morton in Indianapolis from October 1863 until February 1865. The prominent New York physician, who would serve a term as president of the American Medical Association, entitled his lengthy piece in the national periodical, "Cold Cheer at Camp Morton."

Wyeth's was a firsthand and often shocking and explicit account of starvation, exposure to extreme cold and heat, beatings by prison guards, and even coldhearted murder of innocent prisoners within the confines of this Northern prison complex.

Citizens of Indianapolis, the state of Indiana, and the magazine's readership throughout the nation were no doubt greatly disturbed by Wyeth's compelling story about what he had seen and experienced at Camp Morton.

"I have waited to publish this unhappy experience until a quarter of a century has elapsed since it happened," he wrote in the article. "The Southern side of prison life has not yet been fully written. My comrades died by the hundreds amid healthful surroundings [in the

Indianapolis community . . . there was] little cause for death had humane and reasonable care of the prisoners been exercised."[1]

"Cold Cheer" painted a bleak and utterly disturbing and appalling picture of a Northern prison that had, until the time of Wyeth's article, enjoyed a reputation as one of the most humane Northern prisons used to hold Confederate prisoners during the Civil War.

In the final paragraph of "Cold Cheer," Wyeth quoted official War Department records at that time as showing that 1,762 of 12,082 prisoners who were confined to Camp Morton—or 14.6 percent—perished. The records Wyeth quoted indicated that 11.7 percent of all Confederates in Northern prisons died. Wyeth's statistics may have even been a little too conservative, since some historians believe that as many as two thousand Confederate soldiers may have actually perished at Camp Morton (some estimates place the total number of Rebels who passed through Camp Morton between 1861 and 1865 at close to fifteen thousand).

Not surprisingly, Wyeth's charges of callous indifference to human suffering and outright cruelty suffered by the imprisoned Rebels in Indianapolis were met with great indignation by the citizens there—especially the Union military heroes of the community.

Trying to quickly undo the damage to the Hoosier state's reputation done by the Wyeth revelations, the Department Encampment of the Grand Army of the Republic organized a committee to "investigate the statements made" by Wyeth in his controversial article.

Among the members of this GAR committee was no less than Lew Wallace, a prominent Union military officer during the Civil War who gained international fame as the author of the classic American novel *Ben-Hur*.

This group of distinguished Hoosiers appointed W. R. Holloway, a Civil War-era secretary to Indiana governor Oliver P. Morton (for whom Camp Morton was named), to prepare a "paper" to be submitted to *Century Monthly Magazine* as an official rebuttal to Wyeth's charges.

Holloway, who still lived in Indianapolis at the time of the Camp Morton controversy, wrote that during the Civil War Morton had assigned him to visit "all of the camps" and to "learn something of their management."

Holloway contended that, as a part of fulfilling his orders from Morton, he talked with prisoners at Camp Morton "almost daily." He reported that he "visited their barracks, ate their food, and saw their

Indiana's Lew Wallace played a major role in the Camp Morton controversy and publicly defended the treatment of Confederate soldiers at the prison. Wallace wrote the classic novel Ben-Hur. *Photo from the National Archives.*

bread baked in a bakery." Holloway lavishly defended his former boss, a popular Indiana political leader of his time, saying of Morton: "His nature was brave and generous and his heart was as tender as that of a woman."[2]

Century Monthly Magazine agreed to publish Holloway's lengthy response to Wyeth's assertions and "A Reply to 'Cold Cheer at Camp Morton'" appeared it in its September 1891 issue. The controversy was far from over. In fact, it had only just begun.

In the same issue, *Century Monthly* allowed Wyeth an opportunity to answer Holloway's assertions with a "rejoinder." In this piece, Wyeth called on a number of former prisoners, most of them successful and prominent men, to substantiate his charges against Camp Morton.

Wyeth also obtained statements backing his assertions from citizens of Indianapolis, and even Dr. W. P. Parr, assistant surgeon of the United States Army, authored a lengthy first-person account of what he witnessed at Camp Morton that confirmed many of Wyeth's claims.

In time, other Confederate veterans came to Wyeth's defense publicly, including J. K. Womack, who wrote a scathing article in the December 1898 issue of the widely circulated *Confederate Veteran* magazine, calling Camp Morton "that den of misery a little north of Indianapolis."[3]

But John Allan Wyeth, M.D., LL.D., may have not even needed others to come to his defense to substantiate his credibility. Wyeth's reputation was, by any estimation, impeccable and quite secure.

Wyeth joined the Southern cause in the spring of 1862, when he volunteered in Quirk's Scouts, the advance guard of John Hunt Morgan's Confederate raiders. Captain Quirk, assessing seventeen-year-old Wyeth as too immature to fight, had refused his enlistment yet allowed him to ride along. A summer of skirmishing helped to mature "Young Johnny," as he was known to the regiment.

That December, Morgan launched his "Christmas Raid," in which Morgan and his Kentucky horsemen wreaked such damage on the Louisville & Nashville Railroad that it was rendered essentially inoperable for five straight weeks.

On Christmas afternoon, Quirk and his scouts encountered a formation of Federal cavalry and, without properly assessing the situation, charged upon them only to discover too late that they had plunged into an ambush. Quirk and Wyeth, cut off from the others,

A youthful John A. Wyeth is shown wearing his Confederate uniform. Photo from Documenting the American South (http://docsouth.unc.edu), The University of North Carolina at Chapel Hill Libraries.

scrambled for cover and found themselves targets of Yankees firing on them from about forty yards away.

Quirk suffered two head wounds and was bleeding profusely. He ordered Wyeth to run off and find his men, before he, Quirk, was forced to "shoot the damned last one" of the Yankees himself. Wyeth slipped off, made his way to the rear, and soon returned with enough Confederate riders to surround the Federals and force their surrender.

The following year, in October of 1863, after months of skirmishing, scouting, and raiding in central Tennessee, Wyeth—now a bona-fide private in Colonel Russell's Fourth Alabama Cavalry—was able to survive another difficult situation. At Shelbyville, thrown from his horse, he had to lie among the dead as Union cavalry rode over him.

In the Sequatchie Valley, during a raid on a Federal wagon train, he and two companions found themselves cut off and all but surrounded by Federal troopers. Dropping from their horses, they eluded the Union cavalry and made their escape along a wooded ridge.

Two days later, Wyeth's good fortune finally ran out. Cresting another ridge, Wyeth and other Confederates found themselves face to face with a company of cavalry. They were taken prisoner and, later in the day, turned over to the Tenth Illinois Infantry.[4]

Soon afterwards, Wyeth was shipped by train to the Union prison at Camp Morton, Indiana, where he was incarcerated for the next sixteen months of his young life. No doubt, Wyeth left Confederate service as a man after having entered the army as a wet-behind-the-ears youth.

At the end of the Civil War, Wyeth went home to the South and earned a medical degree. He went on to found the New York Polyclinic Medical School and Hospital, the pioneer organization during his time for postgraduate medical instruction in America.

Wyeth served as president of the American Medical Association and scholarly works he authored about surgery and anatomy won prizes from the AMA. He also wrote some well-received books on American history, including an account of his experiences during the Civil War.

An obvious question begs to be answered about Dr. Wyeth's campaign to shine the spotlight of public opinion on the unsavory events at Camp Morton during the Civil War. Why did this distinguished medical scientist wait until more than a quarter-century had passed to drop his bombshell on Indianapolis, the state of Indiana, and the rest of the nation?

Wyeth answered that question succinctly in his "Cold Cheer" article. He said that he believed an unfairness existed in the postwar nation's perception of how Union prisoners were treated versus the treatment of Confederate prisoners. And as is the case with many veterans of armed conflict and imprisonment during wartime, Wyeth probably also needed the passage of twenty-five years to make his memories of Camp Morton less painful and traumatic to remember and recount.

Many Confederate veterans in the years and decades following the Great Conflict felt they had suffered severe humiliation at the hands of the Union government and military. They had not only been soundly defeated, but their homeland had been pillaged in the process.

While many in the Northern states believed that the Civil War was fought primarily over the moral issue of the institution of slavery, most Southern veterans saw it otherwise. They believed that they fought in the many bloody battles of the war for "States' Rights" and to protect their homes and families from invading Union armies. The Confederate soldier believed that his cause was a noble one and he was willing to kill and, if necessary, die for it.

The Confederate Nation's reputation had been greatly damaged by stories of horrific treatment of Union prisoners in makeshift Southern prisons like the infamous Andersonville facility. Wyeth simply believed it was time to tell the other side of the story.

In Wyeth's "Rejoinder" in *Century Monthly Magazine,* Texas congressman and ex-Rebel C. B. Kilgore undoubtedly spoke for thousands of Confederate veterans when he said:

> Controversies which tend to engender bad feelings are much to be deplored, but exact justice should be done to both sides. Every ugly phase of the Southern prisons has been frequently made public. They were bad enough in all conscience, and neither side can scarcely justify the treatment given to prisoners of war.[5]

The Camp Morton controversy had been long forgotten by most citizens in Indianapolis and Indiana when a military base in Johnson County in central Indiana played "host" to prisoners captured during a time of war. In this case, the relatively small number of prisoners were Germans and Italians captured by U.S. forces during World War II.

Just prior to World War II, two Indianapolis schoolteachers and historians, Hattie Lou Winslow and Joseph R. H. Moore, undertook the ambitious project of documenting the entire history of Camp Morton. *Camp Morton 1861-1865* was published by the Indiana Historical Society in 1940.

In the book's foreword, Christopher B. Coleman, the society's secretary, made mention of the Camp Morton controversy when he wrote, "At various times there has been controversy over the treatment and condition of the prisoners kept at Camp Morton. The authors have attempted to give a fair and objective treatment of the subject and to provide an honest picture of the life of the camp."[6]

But the authors of *Camp Morton,* a generally well researched and well written historical document, devoted only a half-page to the Camp Morton controversy. Perhaps during those heady days of pre-World War II patriotism and nationalism, the authors judged that criticism of the behavior of Indiana military and civic leaders during the Civil War might not be well received. Perhaps they also did not want to offend and embarrass the living sons and daughters of those same leaders.

Hattie Lou Winslow and Joseph R. H. Moore researched their book primarily by studying newspapers published in Indianapolis during the Civil War era. When it came to documenting the severe hardship and abuse suffered by the Confederate soldiers at Camp Morton, the local newspapers were mostly silent.

The authors wrote, "The Indianapolis newspapers contain very little information about what was going on at Camp Morton at this time, aside from one or two mentions of abnormally cold weather and mentions of the arrival and departures of prisoners. Outsiders were rigidly excluded from the Camp."[7]

So while certainly not ignoring the problems and resulting controversy associated with Camp Morton, the authors did not explore those issues in any real depth. The book was basically a scholarly undertaking to record the history of the camp for future generations—no more, no less.

Since *Camp Morton 1861-1865,* this author can find no national document of consequence about the Camp Morton controversy (though a few Web sites devoted to the camp and its history make mention of it).

The Camp Morton controversy has, for the most part, remained forgotten and ignored by the public and historians for well over a century.

Century Monthly Magazine's editors cancelled a proposed sequel to "Cold Cheer," but Dr. Wyeth refused to back down, taking every additional opportunity to, as one historian has said, "make public the grim accounts and chilling statistics the North didn't care to hear."

Wrote old Dr. Wyeth: "Facts are cold and unanswerable. And dead men *do* tell tales."

Camp Morton was named for Indiana governor Oliver P. Morton, shown here in a formal portrait. Photo from the National Archives.

CHAPTER 2

Under the Shade
of Walnuts and Oaks

Samuel Henderson, the first mayor of Indianapolis, originally owned the thirty-six-acre tract of land to the north of the city that would become Camp Morton. In those early years of the nineteenth century, this area known as either "Henderson's Grove" or "Otis' Grove" was a place for quiet walks in the country and picnics under the shade of towering black walnut and oak trees.

Since Henderson was known to be a friendly man, he made the grove open to many of the citizenry in Indianapolis. Along with the family picnics, it became a favorite place for local Methodists to hold their camp meetings.

Henderson's Grove, located in what is now an inner-city area on the near north side of Indianapolis, marked the northern limit of civilization during the early and mid-1800s. It had four good springs. A creek flowing through the property was usually dry in the summer. But when the spring rains came, it often became a turbulent stream, overrunning its banks.

Local officials decided that a large ditch was needed to accommodate the water from this relatively small creek. After the creek was dredged in 1837, it became known as State Ditch and later was nicknamed the "Potomac" by Confederate prisoners at Camp Morton.

In 1859, the state of Indiana took possession of the Henderson's Grove acreage in order to construct a State Fairgrounds facility. By 1861, there were several buildings on the grounds, and stables had been constructed to house livestock. On the north side were long, open-ended, shedlike structures for horses. The west end of the grounds contained stalls for 250 cattle as well as sheds for sheep and hogs and an exhibition hall. A large dining hall was on the east

27

end, and a two-story office building stood near the center of the Fairgrounds.[1] But the new State Fairgrounds would not stay a fair-grounds for public use for very long.

After cannons boomed down South and Fort Sumter fell in April 1861, recruiting stations were opened in Indianapolis in response to Pres. Abraham Lincoln's call for Union volunteers. Indiana gov-ernor Oliver P. Morton appointed Lew Wallace to the position of adjutant general. Wallace, a native Hoosier, would go on to lead a fascinating life. After service as a combat officer in the Civil War, he participated in trials of the Lincoln assassination conspirators and Henry Wirz, commandant of Andersonville prison camp. He pub-lished the American classic novel *Ben-Hur* in 1880.

Governor Morton was a staunch advocate for the Union cause, in a state that had many pockets of "butternuts" (Confederate sympa-thizers). When the Civil War broke out, Morton quickly demon-strated his commitment to defend the Union. Immediately, with the aid of Wallace, 6,000 soldiers were raised to answer Lincoln's first call for men. Throughout the war, Indiana met every call for more men. Morton mobilized the war effort in Indiana by raising money, implementing the production of military equipment, and helping to maintain civilian morale.

During the war, Morton would come to be called "the soldiers' friend" for his support of Union troops. He made a special effort to supply Hoosier soldiers with what they needed to fight the Rebels and remain alive in the process.

Governor Morton and Wallace began to survey the small, but growing, town of Indianapolis to find a suitable location where the new Union volunteers could be trained in the military arts. They decided that the State Fairgrounds was the only suitable place in the city. On April 17, 1861, Camp Morton was hastily put into oper-ation and received its first Union volunteers.

To accommodate the anticipated influx of Yankee volunteers, workers set out to construct more sheds to serve as barracks. Each one of the barracks was constructed with the idea of holding about 320 men. They were built of green lumber, with four tiers of bunks set against two sides of the shed, extending seven feet towards the middle so that the men slept perpendicular to the wall. Situated between the two rows of bunks were long dining tables.

The camp was surrounded by a high board fence around which armed guards would be stationed when the camp later began receiving Confederate prisoners. As more and more Union volunteers flooded into the camp, the barracks were supplemented with tents.

The local companies of Guards and Zouaves were the very first Union troops to arrive in the camp. Men and boys from throughout Indiana began to arrive daily and were formed into regiments and companies as fast as they were assembled.

Some of the poor Indiana farm boys came to the camp barefooted and wearing threadbare clothing. But these first regiments of Indiana soldiers were said to have become well drilled and well uniformed in time.[2]

Troop drills were first attempted within the confines of the camp, but the many buildings and trees made this task difficult. City military officials then acquired an area just south of the camp (which had by then been named Camp Morton, in honor of the Indiana governor), and this became a suitable place for the training drills and parading.

Diversity was not a consideration in those days. Two Irish regiments and a German regiment were formed because Union officials deemed it "wise not to mix nationalities." But in time, all of the troops began to adjust to the facilities and to the daily activities and discipline of camp life.[3]

The public in Indianapolis soon became fascinated with the camp. This was an age when little in the way of entertainment was available. There were no radios or TVs or movie theaters, and the telephone had not yet been invented.

Roads leading to the camp became filled with horse-drawn vehicles, especially during the weekends, when it was fashionable to drive one's carriage out to the site. The "hack" (horse-drawn carriage) business thrived in Indianapolis, thanks to the public interest in the camp. Ten cents earned a customer a ride in a hack to the camp from the downtown Circle in Indianapolis and back.

Sunday became the most popular day for those trips. It was estimated that on one day in the spring of 1861, as many as 10,000 visitors came to the camp. When added to the 5,000 soldiers training there, Camp Morton became a veritable "city within a city" that day. The Sunday following this deluge of visitors, the camp was finally ordered closed to outsiders, much to the disappointment of the Indianapolis citizenry.[4]

Another event involving Camp Morton during that period created a major stir in Indianapolis and throughout Indiana. Rumors began to swell that Stephen A. Douglas, a political "superstar" of his time, was coming to speak at the camp. State legislators marched as a body to Camp Morton, preceded by the National Guard Band. The city filled with excitement about the approaching appearance of the great political orator.

Douglas had been a losing candidate for the Democratic presidential nomination in 1852 and 1856. In the presidential campaign of 1860, Abraham Lincoln was the Republican candidate. The Northern states strongly supported him, but the Southern states were split among several candidates, including Douglas, John Cabell Breckinridge, and John Bell.

In 1858, Lincoln had run against Douglas for a seat in the U.S. Senate. The two men engaged in a series of famous debates during this campaign, which established Lincoln's skill at public speaking and were also partly responsible for getting him elected to the presidency two years later.

When seven states from the deep South seceded from the U.S. in 1861, Douglas searched for a compromise that would save the Union. Once the Civil War began, he pledged his support to President Lincoln and the fight to preserve the Union.

With the roads to Camp Morton becoming virtually packed with people awaiting Douglas's much-anticipated appearance, his carriage driver could not even get close to the site. There was no speech, much to the disappointment of thousands of Hoosiers, and Douglas was finally obliged to escape by a side road to rejoin his party.[5] In June 1861, weakened by years of overwork and excessive drinking, Douglas would die while on a trip to secure Illinois's support for the Union cause.

Yet while Douglas was escaping the chaos at Camp Morton, a rumor began to circulate among the crowd who had come to see him that the camp's wells had been poisoned and that a peddler had been selling poisoned oranges at the camp. Military officials responded to this bogus report by posting more guards at the wells. Amusingly, a "Dr. Fletcher" enjoyed his fifteen minutes of fame when he heroically stopped a mounting riot by publicly eating one of the "libeled" oranges.

Governor Morton and Indiana military officials had seen enough by this time. In the aftermath of the Douglas debacle, they issued

Stephen A. Douglas, a superstar politician of his time, was supposed to give a speech at Camp Morton prior to its being used as a prison, but the throngs of people wanting to see him prevented his appearance. Photo from the National Archives.

orders to tighten discipline and to restore more of a military atmosphere to Camp Morton.[6]

Union soldiers sequestered at the camp spent much of their time drilling and parading, but they still found time for entertainment. Some brought games from home, such as checkers, chess, and playing cards. Others found enjoyment in rougher "games," such as a boisterous activity known as the "Knights of Malta Initiation." In this activity, the unfortunate soldier getting "initiated" was tossed repeatedly on a tent canvas by a group of his peers.

In general, the Union soldiers' basic needs were cared for while they were training in the camp, though, by modern standards, they certainly did not live in comfort. The Ladies' Patriotic Association, organized by Governor Morton's wife, collected blankets, socks, gloves, and mittens for the soldiers. But soldiers still criticized the clothing supplies during the cold winter months. Many of the items collected by the well-intentioned women, most made of inferior wool, were said to be shoddy and did not stand up to the rigors of military camp.

There was a delay in providing sorely needed overcoats to the soldiers. They were forced to go without them for a time while a frustrated Governor Morton wrangled with Union military bureaucrats.

The quality of food available at the camp often drew strong complaints from the young Union soldiers. And many of their complaints appear to have been well founded. Due to supply problems, there was a very limited amount of canned goods. Most of the time, the "menu" for the Union soldiers would include items such as salted meats (of varying degrees of saltiness), salted fish, some fruit, and some vegetables.

When these soldier complaints began to be circulated among the public at large, boxes flooded into the camp from the soldiers' homes, containing such delicacies as roasted fowl, baked ham, fresh butter and eggs, jellies, pound cakes, and other sweet favorites.

The camp became plagued by a constant turnover of supervisory military officials. Most competent officers wanted to be out fighting Confederates and did not appreciate an assignment of training soldiers in Indiana.

This caused a succession of higher officers to go to the field of battle. Replacements had to be provided from officers new to the work of military training. The young Union soldiers being trained at the camp found plenty to complain about concerning the supervisory staff when writing letters home.[7]

Within a relatively short time, the tract of land north of the city of Indianapolis had gone from being a popular picnic spot, to the site of the State Fairgrounds, to a training camp for young Union soldiers and a tourist attraction for thousands of Hoosiers.

But the major history-making developments at this property had just begun. Samuel Henderson would have likely never dreamt that his pristine farm acreage, shaded by oak and walnut trees and blessed with flowing springs and a creek, would one day play host to thousands of Union soldiers and tourists.

And the affable former mayor of Indianapolis would have certainly never imagined that his pleasant farmland grove would one day become the site of terrible pain, suffering, degradation, and even death for thousands of young men who had come to this place from the far-off Southern land called the American Confederacy.

CHAPTER 3

Early Days of the Prison

Indianapolis had reluctantly agreed to receive a few Confederate prisoners in the early months of the Civil War, but the community really did not know what to do with them.

Sometimes, if prisoners had financial means, they were allowed to live at a hotel, reporting to military officials once a day. Those without money were allowed to get jobs in the city and use the income for their support.

But after the fall of Fort Henry and Fort Donelson in February 1862, these casual arrangements quickly changed. Governor Morton, in response to a telegraph from Union general Henry Halleck, agreed to accept up to three thousand prisoners to be head-quartered at Indianapolis's Camp Morton.

The monumental job of converting a military camp into a prison camp fell to Capt. James A. Ekin, an assistant quartermaster general of the U.S. Army. He directed work to erect additional barracks, and some were not completed until after the first prisoners began arriving.

The first group of these Confederates, arriving in Indianapolis on February 22, 1862, were greeted with much excitement, interest, and curiosity throughout the city. Within the next few days, 3,700 captured Rebels would be sent to Camp Morton. Governor Morton drew from several partially filled Indiana regiments to guard these men. He appointed Col. Richard Owen commandant of the prison.[1]

From the outset, Colonel Owen had his hands full. Many of the prisoners were in poor health, some with life-threatening illness. The *Indianapolis Journal* described the condition of the newly arrived prisoners as follows:

Of the sick prisoners at the military prison and hospitals of this city, the greater proportion are Mississippians. Though some of the Tennesseans and Kentuckians are quite ill, their maladies are not so deep-seated as those of . . . the Mississippi prisoners. These regiments were at Fort Henry and, at the time of the attack, . . . retreated so rapidly that they left behind most of their baggage, including many articles of clothing much-needed for their comfort and protection against the elements.

On arriving at Fort Donelson, they were put at work immediately upon the fortifications and were compelled to labor upon the trenches constantly.

During the siege of the Fort, they would lay in the ditches and rifle pits, day and night. Such exposure would produce disease in the ranks of the most able-bodied soldiers, but when incurred by men of feeble constitutions, the seeds of disease are so firmly planted that no medical skill can remove them.

Of the latter class are those now in hospitals. Many are under eighteen years of age, and the large majority are persons of feeble constitution. They receive the best medical treatment, and the nursing care of female attendants; but in many cases the best of attention cannot save them from the grasp of death.[2]

Various locations throughout Indianapolis were used to provide hospital care for the ill Confederate prisoners. Despite the dedicated and compassionate efforts of the hospitals' staff workers, many patients died due to the poor conditions they were in when they arrived at Indianapolis.

John K. Farris, a Confederate physician who served with the Forty-first Tennessee Volunteers, was among the Confederate soldiers who came to Camp Morton after having been captured at Fort Donelson. Soon after his imprisonment in February 1862, he wrote a poem to his wife, Mary, describing his feelings about being separated from his family and friends who were waiting for him back in the hills of Tennessee:

It is awful, 'tis awful a prisoner to be
And think of my home in old Tennessee—
A wife and a child who to me are so near
And yet not a word from them can I hear.[3]

By April 1, 1862, there were an estimated five thousand men in camp, including the guards. Prisoners continued to arrive during the spring and summer of 1862, including an estimated one thousand Confederate prisoners brought in after the battle of Shiloh.[4]

Colonel Owen was proving to be an able administrator and he was generally liked by both guards and prisoners. An experienced soldier who combined strength and gentleness, Owen was a disciplinarian but tempered his discipline with grace and mercy. He said that his goal as administrator at the prison was to treat the prisoners in a way "calculated to make them less restless in their confinement, and likely, when they returned to their homes, to spread among their friends and acquaintances the news that they had been deceived regarding [the character of] Northern men."[5]

Because no federal regulations had been written for the treatment of prisoners, Owen established "Eleven Rules" for the humane and common-sense treatment of prisoners. The last rule most represented Owen's overall approach to running the camp: "Every endeavor will be made by the commandant to give each and every prisoner as much liberty and comfort as is consistent with orders received and with an equal distribution of the means at disposal, provided such indulgence never leads to any abuse of the privileges."[6]

Colonel Owen's Eleven Rules established a virtual self-government among the prisoners. Sometimes townspeople complained that the rules were too liberal, but Owen's measured approach earned appreciation from most of the prisoners.

During the first somewhat disorganized months of the prison's use, noncommissioned Confederate officers in charge of companies were nearly as busy as Colonel Owen. Besides requisitioning the proper amount of rations for the men, they had the somewhat difficult duty of fairly dividing out the food.

The slightest perceived partiality provoked major controversy among the prisoner ranks. Because a few of the prisoners were willing to steal food from their comrades, cooks had to stand guard over it. Honest men developed a habit of immediately eating their whole day's ration or of carrying it in their haversacks for safekeeping.

· Colonel Owen allowed prisoners to receive supplies of clothing from home, but many of these garments were not practical for prison-camp usage. One soldier was not very happy with the embroidered slippers he received from his girlfriend back home.[7]

It fell on the Federal government to provide most of the clothing and other supplies for the prisoners. They received clothing that had been furnished to the government by contractors but that the government inspectors had then condemned. Many times, those "condemned" items were not what the prisoners most needed. Or, shipments were delayed.

Much to the disappointment of prisoners and their loved ones in nearby Southern states, Governor Morton ruled immediately that outsiders would not have access to the prisoners, even relatives and friends. He did not make this decision for punitive reasons, but rather to secure Camp Morton against potential sabotage from outside forces.

However, communication from home by mail was allowed. All material contributed to the camp locally, such as newspapers and books, had to be examined by guards for fear that weapons or tools might be concealed between the pages. Money, clothing, and other donations were normally allowed in after proper inspection.

In general, sutlers (traveling merchants) were not permitted to sell their wares to the prisoners. However, Colonel Owen loosened up this regulation for peddlers of books and periodicals. He said that it was "beneficial to the prisoners by keeping them occupied and contented." Owen also secured several hundred books for the men from the state's Department of Public Instruction.[8]

Colonel Owen allowed the soldiers the enjoyable pastime of listening to music. Though camp regulations discouraged the prisoners from congregating in groups of more than two or three at a time—especially at night—they were permitted to form glee clubs.

A band of "Ethiopian minstrels" gave concerts from time to time. On one occasion, some prisoners serenaded fellow prisoners and camp staff with "Dixie" and a collection of other songs popular among Confederate soldiers during the Civil War.

Along with the singing, young men in the camp who had developed talent as thespians prior to the war were allowed to arrange dramatic entertainment programs to present to their hospitalized comrades. One of these talented young Confederate soldiers reportedly took the oath of allegiance, became a member of the old Metropolitan Company, and remained in Indianapolis for years after the war.[9]

During the spring of 1862, John Martin Wood wrote a letter from Camp Morton to his wife, Helen. He was a Confederate prisoner from Giles County, Tennessee. In his letter, Wood sought to calm the fears of his young wife by telling her that his needs were being met at Camp Morton. He painted a rather rosy a picture, perhaps to make his wife feel more secure, even mentioning that the captives enjoyed playing "baste ball." He wrote:

> I know that our [separation] is bitter. But we must put up with it as best we can and hope for the better and I do hope my dear, that henceforth you will not allow your spirits to be so depressed on my account. For I am doing well under existing circumstances.
>
> Our encampment is a beautiful place. The walls of which contain about 40 acres on which we exercise ourselves by playing baste ball . . . and I have as good well water as I ever drank.[10]

The popular Colonel Owen did not stay camp commandant for very long. In late May 1862, he was called into active duty. Governor Morton appointed Col. David Garland Rose as the commandant to follow Colonel Owen.

During this time, replacement guards volunteered from throughout Indiana. By the end of the first week of June, over four hundred such guards had been sworn in for three months' service.

This continuous shifting of guard companies caused some problems at Camp Morton, because many of the soldiers were young and inexperienced. Some were even reported to have accidentally wounded themselves with firearms.

Colonel Rose was, in many ways, the opposite of Colonel Owen in personality and in philosophy about his new position. He was a strict administrator and some prisoners grew to dislike him to the point of hatred. On July 14, twenty-five prisoners tried to escape during a stormy Hoosier night. All but one of these escapees were found and returned to camp.[11]

John K. Farris was likely commenting on this episode in a letter he wrote home dated July 27, 1862. In poetic language, he described the difficulty of trying to escape. "On prison walls we all are bound, with soldiers all outside. Their drums do beat and bugles sound, if to escape be tried."[12]

A few incidents involved Confederate prisoners who strayed too close to the camp walls. One was shot after he was reportedly given the required "three warnings" by a guard.[13]

One has to wonder if Farris, who would soon have many reasons to be thankful to his Maker, had any idea he would be leaving the prison in a matter of only a few weeks when he wrote the following message home in early August 1862: "This is the first preaching we have ever had in our company since we have been in service, and I believe it is the first sermon I have heard, though it is my own fault, for we have had a good deal of preaching in this prison since here by both soldiers of our own army and citizens of Indianapolis."[14]

In late August, after both Union and Confederate military leaders agreed to a prisoner exchange, 1,280 Confederate prisoners left Camp Morton and Indianapolis amid a large crowd of curious local spectators. Other prisoners left in groups over the next six days, until the only prisoners who remained were those whose names did not appear on any rolls, or sick prisoners and their nurses.

The ill prisoners were later discharged during the first week of September. By this time, Camp Morton was emptied of all Confederate prisoners and an immediate "renovation and purification" was begun by companies from the Fifth Cavalry.

Starting in late September 1862, 3,000 paroled Union prisoners arrived at Camp Morton. By November 17, after having been formally exchanged, they were freed to service. By early December, Camp Morton was nearly empty.[15]

But it would not remain so for long.

CHAPTER 4

Darkness Falls on Camp Morton

When the parole system temporarily cleared out Camp Morton, many local officials probably thought that the camp's days as a Civil War prison were over for good. As it turned out, the parole system did not last long and neither did the inactivity at the camp.

The parole system was initiated when the North and South governments, at a loss as to how to deal with large numbers of captured troops early in the war, negotiated to adopt the traditional European system of parole and exchange of prisoners. The new system's terms called for prisoners to promise not to take up arms against their captors until they were formally exchanged for an enemy captive of equal rank. Parole was supposed to take place within ten days of capture. Generally, it was granted within a few days, especially after a major battle. Sometimes parolees could temporarily return home to await notice of their exchange; sometimes they waited near their commands until all paperwork was completed.

As the war progressed and numbers of parolees mounted, the parole system grew increasingly complex, cumbersome, and expensive.

The prospect of being sent home encouraged many men to place themselves in a position where they could be easily captured in battle or by "straggling." Some parolees were permanently lost to an army when they failed to return to their units.

Detention camps established by Federal authorities angered parolees, as did attempts to use them as guards, send them West to do battle with Indians, or give them noncombat assignments. Technically, paroled troops could not be assigned any duty that would free other soldiers for combat.

Confederate prisoners captured in Virginia are lined up by Union troops to make a long trip to a prison somewhere in the North. Photo from the National Archives.

More Confederate troops captured in Virginia await being sent to a Union prison. Some sprawl out on the ground; others can be seen building fires. Photo from the National Archives.

Many glaring problems surfaced in the system. Soldiers assigned to detention camps frequently suffered from shortages of food and clothing and poor sanitation, and some were victimized by their own comrades. Union authorities generally withheld parole and exchange from prisoners who were identified as guerrillas, bush-whackers, and blockade runners. This resulted in retaliatory action by the Confederacy.

Recognizing that the war was being prolonged by returning men to the ranks through parole and exchange (which by 1863 was the Confederate Army's primary means of maintaining troop strength), Federal authorities severely restricted the program. The alternative, confining captured enemy troops to prison camps, then became accepted policy.[1]

Camp Morton had been essentially emptied out by the parole system in early winter 1862. Within a few months after the Confederate prisoners left, vacant buildings at the camp began to fall into disrepair. But by the end of January 1863, prisoners were once more streaming into Camp Morton, two to three hundred at a time. A new commandant came on the scene during this time, Col. James Biddle.

Confederate prisoners at Camp Morton are shown here building small fires to try to keep warm. Photo from the Indiana Historical Society.

A thorough renovation and rebuilding was needed at Camp Morton during the first months of 1863, but nothing of consequence was done to improve the its dilapidated state. This is how the authors of *Camp Morton 1861-1865,* described its condition:

> For two years, Union recruits and Confederate prisoners had crowded the barracks and swarmed over the enclosure. The buildings, which dated from the camp's fairgrounds days, had been put to every use but the intended ones, and the few which had been erected since the beginning of the war were flimsy makeshifts designed on the theory that the war would soon be over.
>
> Nothing had been done in anticipation of a probable need and by the time the necessity of improvement was acknowledged, weeks and months of delay had usually aggravated the need to [double] its original proportions. From 1863 until 1865, the record contains a sorry round of inspectors' complaints and recommendations, and orders from the Commissary General of Prisoners in which permission for improvement was always balanced by the strictest exhortation to economy.[2]

Early on July 8, 1863, Confederate brigadier general John Hunt Morgan and 2,000 cavalrymen crossed the Ohio River into Indiana, causing a great stir among Hoosiers in southern Indiana as well as in central Indiana and Indianapolis. Morgan's cavalry raiders crossed into Indiana from Kentucky, using two captured steamboats. For six days, the raiders rode through southern Indiana.

Upon landing in Indiana, Morgan headed north and Indianapolis residents began to fear that his destination was their city. Facing only relatively small resistance, Morgan camped five miles north of the Ohio River on July 8. The Battle of Corydon (Indiana) occurred the next day as Morgan's men eventually outflanked the 450 men of the home guard in the small town. Morgan left Corydon on the afternoon of July 9.

Throughout Morgan's raid, his men spread out from the main column, pillaging as they traveled. The railroad and telegraph were primary targets of destruction. Food and fresh horses were in constant demand by Morgan's troopers and they were taken from the homes of farmers along the route. Brave, but inexperienced, Indiana militia troops were unable to stop Morgan and his men. However, the situation was about to change.

A Union cavalry force of about four thousand Yankees under the command of Brig. Gen. Edward Hobson began to pursue Morgan. These troops crossed the Ohio River from Kentucky on July 10 and were within twenty-five miles of Morgan's column.

In Indianapolis, Governor Morton issued a call for volunteers to defend the state against Morgan's cavalry. Approximately twenty thousand responded. Thirteen regiments were mustered into service, and Morgan gave command of these regiments to his trusted Hoosier friend, Lew Wallace.

Morgan decided to turn to the east and began to parallel the Ohio River. He entered Lexington, Indiana, late on July 10. The raiders started early the next day towards Paris and Vernon, Indiana, realizing that their enemies were not far behind them and probably in front of them as well.

At the tiny hamlet of Vernon, Indiana, the raiders were actually turned back for the first time by local troops. The home guard of Jennings County had taken up a strong position at Vernon on a bluff overlooking the Muscatatuck River. Morgan decided it would not be to his benefit to confront the Vernon home guard patriots, so he turned southeast towards tiny Dupont, destroying bridges along the way.

Morgan's raiders arrived in Versailles on July 12 and robbed the county treasury of $5,000. With much more money in their pockets, the raiders left Versailles and headed northeast.

Early on July 13, Morgan and the raiders resumed their eastward ride. The advance guard of Morgan's cavalrymen crossed a bridge into Harrison, Ohio, in early afternoon. The so-called "Great Raid" would soon come to a close. As the end of Morgan's column made it into Ohio at about 7:00 P.M., they burned one last bridge for good measure.

Hobson's troops continued the chase through Ohio. In late July, the Great Raid came to an end when Morgan was captured in northeastern Ohio with only 364 men.

Prisoners in Camp Morton who had contacts with Confederate sympathizers in Indianapolis learned about Morgan's raid. This information no doubt caused great commotion among the prison population. Most had to be hoping that Morgan would come to Indianapolis, as was rumored, and that this would result in their liberation from the prison and their return to the Confederate Army.

But Morgan's men did not end up coming to the rescue of the

Camp Morton prisoners. Ironically, many of them would end up joining those same prisoners inside the walls of the camp.

An estimated 1,100 of Morgan's men who had been captured during the raid were brought to Camp Morton. Viewed with great curiosity by the other prisoners, many of them came from wealthy and influential families in nearby Kentucky, a fact that apparently carried some weight with Camp Morton officials.

Due to their celebrity, and the slackening of camp discipline under temporary commandants, the new prisoners were allowed visits from friends and relatives. Some of those visitors were reportedly loyal to the Union cause and asked Morgan's men to take the oath of allegiance. There were apparently few takers.[3]

Morgan's raiders, accustomed to deferential treatment all of their young lives due to their wealth and celebrity, began to cause problems in the camp. They made trouble among the other prisoners and participated in quarrels and riots.

Conditions throughout the camp grew steadily worse. Command of the camp continued to be transferred at short intervals, and prison guards were becoming demoralized and undisciplined. Recognizing opportunities left available by uninspired guards, many prisoners began to make plans for escape.

Some groups never made it safely out of the prison. Others were caught soon after they escaped the enclosure. But thirty-five men were able to get safely away between the first part of August and the end of October.[4]

Trying to escape was one of the most popular pastimes at all Civil War prisons, and Camp Morton was no exception. Some attempts were elaborate. Prisoners often feigned sickness or sometimes even death in the hope that they would be carried outside the stockade walls and left for dead. Once outside, the "deceased" prisoners would simply walk away. At Camp Douglas, in Illinois, inmates darkened their skin with charcoal and walked out with the black servants. This particular approach was attempted so many times that wardens abolished the use of African-Americans as prison laborers.

Tunneling was, by far, the most widespread method of escape from Civil War prisons. In one of the most famous prison breaks, known as the "Great Yankee Tunnel," 109 Union prisoners crawled to freedom from Libby Prison in Richmond, Virginia, after digging a sixty-foot tunnel using only clam shells and case knives.

Escape attempts continued throughout the war, but the majority of them failed. Prisoners unlucky enough to be caught were punished severely. Some of the harsh penalties included hard labor, hanging by the thumbs, and other forms of physical and psychological torture. Many prisoners were shot and killed while trying to escape. Despite such possibilities, Union and Confederate POWs continued their attempts to break free.

Prisoners did not plan escapes to pass the time. In many cases, they were simply trying to survive. Previous recent inspections of Camp Morton by Union medical officials had not been complimentary, but a scorching report in late October by Augustus M. Clark raised eyebrows throughout Indianapolis. He called Camp Morton "a disgrace in the name of military prison" and described it as being "filthy in every respect." In his frank report, Clark pointed to poor handling of sewage, inadequate housing space for the prisoners, nearly inedible food, poor hospital facilities, and other major defects in the camp.[5]

But Clark's accusations were basically downplayed by the local government and military officials. As reports were arriving daily of young Hoosier men dying on Civil War battlefields at the hands of Confederates, it was difficult to summon much enthusiasm about making conditions better in a Rebel prison camp.

Days were beginning to darken early at Camp Morton in the fall of 1863.

CHAPTER 5

The Tightrope Walk
at Camp Morton

Col. Ambrose A. Stevens was a battle-scarred war veteran when he received his appointment to head Camp Morton in October 1863. He had served with honor as a lieutenant colonel and colonel with Michigan troops, and he had been wounded at the Battle of Perryville, Kentucky. When the Union military created the Invalid Corps, later the Veteran Reserve Corps, Stevens was appointed major of the Fifth Regiment.

Early in the Civil War, permanently disabled soldiers received medical discharges from the army, but later they remained in the service and performed noncombat duties, relieving more able-bodied soldiers to fight. In 1862, the Union Army allowed chief medical officers to employ "convalescent wounded and feeble men" in a variety of jobs such as cooks, nurses, and hospital attendants. The original concept was to organize the men into detachments, but that approach proved inefficient, and many convalescents did not return to their combat units until after they had recovered.

In April 1863, the U.S. War Department created an Invalid Corps of "worthy disabled officers and men" who were or had been serving in the army. Ridicule influenced the corps to exchange its sky-blue uniform for one similar to those worn by other soldiers.

The corps formed two "battalions": the first for those who could bear arms and perform garrison duty and the second for severely handicapped soldiers fit only for hospital service. Late in the war, the surgeon general took command of the Second Battalion. Like combat units, the Invalid Corps organized officers and men into companies and regiments.

Renamed the "Veteran Reserve Corps" in March of 1864, it was abolished during the summer of 1866. Between 1863 and 1866, more than sixty thousand soldiers served in the organization and performed valuable services, including garrisoning fortifications and quelling the infamous 1863 "Draft Riot" in New York City.[1]

The Invalid Corps regiment in which Ambrose Stevens was an officer was ordered to Indianapolis early in September 1863 to relieve Indiana troops on guard at Camp Morton.[2] After his appointment as Camp Morton's commandant a month later, Stevens may or may not have then anticipated that he would keep this position until the end of the Civil War. Union authorities favored Stevens and his nononsense style of managing the prison. His main focus was preventing uprisings and escape attempts, not striving to make the Confederate prisoners happy.

Unlike a previous Camp Morton commandant, Colonel Owen, whose kindness and compassion had endeared himself to many of the prisoners, Stevens had no interest in making friends there. When Stevens took command, he outlined a plan to improve the prison's hospital and barracks facilities, but the improvements he ended up initiating barely made a dent in the sad conditions that had developed over time.

To try to understand Stevens' behavior and approach towards running the prison, one must take into account the circumstances under which he served as commandant.

Like all prison commandants, Stevens was no doubt greatly influenced by the political climate in the Union at the time. In the middle and late years of the Civil War, reports of terrible conditions at Andersonville and other prisons in the South were reaching the ears of the public in the North. This created a political environment in the North in which many Unionists argued that what was good enough for a Union prisoner was also good enough for a Confederate prisoner. In effect, it amounted to the ancient precept of "an eye for an eye, a tooth for a tooth."

Andersonville holds an especially infamous place in the annals of Civil War prisons and in the history of man's wartime inhumanity to man. In November 1863, Confederate captain W. Sidney Winder was sent to the village of Andersonville in Sumter County, Georgia, to assess the potential of building a prison there for captured Union soldiers. The village's location in the Deep South, the availability of fresh water, and its closeness to the Southwestern Railroad made it an acceptable site for a prison.

Also, the tiny village of Andersonville had a population of less than twenty residents, and those twenty residents were not going be able to create enough of a fuss to stop the Confederate government from pursuing its plans to construct what would be an unpopular facility in any community.

Capt. Richard B. Winder was sent to Andersonville to build the prison. Arriving in late December of 1863, Captain Winder adopted a prison design that encompassed roughly 16.5 acres to hold an estimated ten thousand prisoners. The prison would be rectangular in shape with a small creek flowing nearly through the center of the compound. The prison was given the name Camp Sumter.

Union prisoners began arriving at Andersonville in late February 1864, and by early June the prison population had climbed to 20,000. Confederate officials then decided that a larger prison was necessary, and by mid-June, enlargement work had begun. By August of that year, over 33,000 Union prisoners were crammed into the 26.5-acre prison.

By early September, William T. Sherman's invading Union troops had occupied Atlanta, and the threat of Union raids on Andersonville prompted the transfer of most of the Union prisoners to other camps in Georgia and South Carolina. By mid-November, all but about 1,500 prisoners had been shipped out of Andersonville,

In Andersonville's fifteen months of operation, almost thirteen thousand Union prisoners died there of malnutrition, exposure, and disease. The name Andersonville became synonymous with the worst kinds of atrocities that can be committed against other human beings during a time of war. When Northern newspapers and periodicals published photographs of emaciated Union prisoners, the Northern populace became outraged.[3]

To the contemporary student of the American Civil War, it seems obvious that one consideration could have moderated public feelings of retribution against Southern prisoners. While the Southern states were struggling to provide their fighting troops in the field with even the barest of necessities, the North had relatively ample resources of money and food.

Stevens and other commandants of Northern Civil War prisons were forced to walk a kind of a "tightrope." If they were considered too generous to Confederate prisoners, they would be reprimanded by higher military authorities. If they were considered too restrictive, they would also be reprimanded.

Chilly weather was setting in early in the Hoosier state in the late fall of 1863. Hundreds of additional prisoners packed the wooden sheds that served as barracks, and they overflowed into tents. The early chilly weather that fall would be a portent of things to come during what would be a memorable winter in Indianapolis.

These cold and wet conditions were difficult enough for young men who had come from warmer Southern environs, but most of the new arrivals came into the camp wearing only tattered remnants of the clothes in which they had begun the summer campaign. Some had no shoes to wear.[4]

Not only did new arrivals look forlorn and bedraggled, they were, as one hospital steward said at the time, "as nearly dead as alive." Many were suffering from a variety of serious health problems, including wounds from the battlefield, exhaustion, and malnutrition. Already ailing and wearing little covering in the cold, they were vulnerable to pneumonia, bronchitis, and other types of viral and bacterial infections.[5]

But the incoming Confederate prisoners would not get much relief from Stevens. Union military officials were becoming less inclined to distribute clothing to prisoners, so Stevens assumed that not much would be made available to him at Camp Morton. As a result, he ordered that blankets and clothing would be issued to only the most destitute of the Rebel prisoners.

Some prisoners suffered from scurvy due to a lack of fresh vegetables. The daily food ration per prisoner included three-quarters of a pound of bacon or a pound of fresh beef, a portion of wheat bread, hominy, potatoes, molasses, coffee, tea, sugar, and salt and pepper. Each prisoner generally cooked his own meals or joined a small group of friends for that purpose.[6]

Most of the prisoners came into the camp poor, but some—such as Morgan's raiders, who had come from affluent Southern homes—could afford to buy food and other items from a camp sutler. Also, prisoners were allowed to receive boxes of food from friends and relatives back home. But on December 1, 1863, the Union government—retaliating against the poor treatment of Northern prisoners in Southern prisons—issued an order shutting off both of these privileges.[7]

By the end of December, Union officials decided that conditions for Yankee prisoners had improved sufficiently, and they allowed Confederate prisoners to purchase tobacco, pipes, writing materials, and stamps. But with the cold months of winter setting in, the Camp

Morton prisoners would not be allowed to receive any extra food to strengthen their bodies and improve their resistance to disease.

Though Camp Morton was a prison by definition, it was also considered a "prison camp" because of the open space within its fenced boundaries. But in the early winter months of 1863, a conventional "prison" would actually be built within the walls of the camp. This new prison was a stout structure for that time, with walls, floor, ceiling, and doors all made of two thicknesses of two-inch planking. It had four fifteen-square-foot cells, ventilated by overhead gratings; a main prison room twenty-four by thirty feet; a "dungeon" sixteen feet square; and an office and guardroom twelve by twenty-four feet. In all, sixty prisoners could be lodged in the facility. There were thirty inmates in January 1864. Some of them were bounty jumpers awaiting court martial. Three of these men, found guilty of repeated desertions, were executed on the parade ground near Camp Morton.[8]

While the popular former camp commandant Colonel Owen recognized the need to keep young Confederate soldiers occupied during their confinement—even to the point of allowing them to stage theatrical and musical presentations—Colonel Stevens took a much different position on these matters. Not only were the prisoners denied opportunities for recreation and creative expression, they were not allowed to work within the camp. Lacking any camp duties and struggling to survive in difficult conditions, many young Rebels began devoting more of their time and efforts to developing plans for escape.

Stevens' Veteran Reserves kept a strict watch over the men, and the prisoners recognized this. But when it came to conspiracies to break loose from the prison, Stevens and other Indiana officials believed they had more to worry about than the prisoners themselves. Prior to the Civil War, a secret order known as the "Knights of the Golden Circle" had been organized in the Southern states. Its original purpose was primarily to expand the institution of slavery in the United States. With the outbreak of the war, chapters of this society were organized among Southern sympathizers, first in border states, then spreading northward into Ohio, Indiana, Illinois, and Missouri. In Indiana as well as in other neighboring states, they took the name "Sons of Liberty," and the order secretly grew.

In 1862, according to a report from an investigating grand jury of a United States circuit court, the group had an estimated fifteen thousand members in Indiana, with local "castles" or lodges, and an elaborate system of words, grips, and signals for mutual identification and communication.[9] The group was investigated by a grand jury because of allegations it had interfered with Northern enlistment efforts, encouraged desertion, protected deserters, and resisted the draft of 1862. The group, many Union officials contended at the time, had not been reluctant to use violence in trying to accomplish its goals.

Though Colonel Stevens already had some informants in the camp, concern about the Sons of Liberty made him consider for a time employing professional detectives to monitor conspiratorial activities within the prison.[10]

Guards were pressured to be vigilant in stopping escapes, but this proved to be a difficult assignment. Most of the prisoners were becoming restless and defiant. Some made trouble among their fellow prisoners and openly insulted guards and prison officials. They often hurled stones at guards. Some prisoners particularly enjoyed aiming at and striking a guard's cartridge box, which would knock the sentinel off balance.

Even though Stevens described some of the prisoners "as tough and depraved characters" as he had ever seen, guards were commanded not to respond to insults and or use force against prisoners unless the violence became life threatening.[11]

Trying to tunnel underneath the prison fence was a common (and obvious) strategy of escape pursued by the Camp Morton prisoners. To counter this practice, Stevens ordered twenty feet of space demolished from the barracks facilities nearest the fence and put prisoners to work digging a deep and wide trench.

Though the Confederates complained aggressively about this digging duty—since they were, in effect, helping to prevent their own opportunities for escape—the work went on. By the time they finished and satisfied Colonel Stevens with their work, a sturdy board enclosure had been erected inside the old wall as a further deterrent to tunneling.[12]

Despite all of these measures, some prisoners did actually manage to escape from Camp Morton. One young soldier who failed was a Louisiana native, Goacin Arcemont, who decided he had could no longer bear shivering in the winter cold.[13] He slipped out of his barracks one January night and headed for an angle in the enclosure where prisoners had previously managed to get safely away. But there was no such good fortune for the young Southern soldier. A guard was there to command him to stop and return to his barracks.

Knowing fully well what ignoring such an order would mean, Arcemont stayed where he was and was fatally shot by the guard. Goacin Arcemont had made a decision to accept death rather than to spend one more day in misery at Indiana's Camp Morton.

CHAPTER 6

"Cold Cheer"
and Coldhearted Murder

John A. Wyeth came to Camp Morton on a memorable night in late October 1863. John Wyeth was not a physician then. He was a young Confederate soldier, a captive, who would spend his first night at Camp Morton trying to sleep on cold, hard Indiana soil.

"[I] arrived at Camp Morton about ten o-clock at night," wrote Dr. Wyeth in "Cold Cheer at Camp Morton," his shocking exposé about his experiences in the Northern Civil War prison. "No provision having been made for us, we slept, or tried to sleep, through the cold night, in the open air and upon the ground."[1]

The young Alabama cavalryman came to the camp already ill. Sleeping on the cold soil there certainly did not improve his health. Wyeth was developing pneumonia and, after a delay while the hospital steward waited for another man to die, the youthful Confederate soldier was admitted to a tent within the compound that served as the hospital.

Young John Wyeth was sick and weak and longing for his Southern homeland. But ultimately, he would be fortunate. He would manage to survive his illness, while hundreds of other sick young men would die at Camp Morton.

Had John Wyeth been one of the prisoner casualties at Camp Morton, perhaps the world would have never learned the full truth about what took place within its walls from 1863 until the end of the Civil War.

Many other Rebel veterans who had been held at Camp Morton would speak out after Wyeth made public his revelations in the April 1891 issue of *Century Monthly*. Wyeth had built a prestigious reputation in the intervening twenty-five years as a prominent physician and medical researcher. Other historic accounts about the later years of Camp Morton deal only superficially with the suffering, pain, and degradation young Rebel prisoners experienced there. But Wyeth's account gave the world a prisoner's-eye view. And what he revealed was startling and horrific in many respects.

A half-century later, the authors of *Camp Morton 1861-1865*, while certainly not strongly endorsing or supporting Wyeth's claims, acknowledged that his stories about life in the camp had, in their opinions, at least some basis for credibility. They wrote: "Where the 'Official Records' cover the material of which [Wyeth] speaks—for example the condition of barracks, hospitals and clothing issues—they tend to substantiate his claims."[2]

After young John Wyeth, the new prisoner, had recovered enough from his life-threatening illness to join his comrades in the regular barracks at Camp Morton, he soon discovered that his living quarters were barely sufficient to shelter animals during the frigid Northern winter months. Following is his description of his temporary home in Indianapolis:

> Camp Morton was, in 1863, a plot of ground formerly used as a fairground, in shape a parallelogram, containing, as well as I could estimate, about twenty acres of land, inclosed [*sic*] by a plank wall about twenty feet high. In its long axis, this plot was bisected by a little rivulet, which the prisoners christened the "Potomac." On each side of this branch the barracks were situated.
>
> These barracks had been erected as cattle sheds and stables. They were about twenty feet wide, in height ten feet to the eaves, fifteen feet to the middle of the roof, and eighty feet long. The sides were of weather-boards ten to twelve inches wide, set on end and presumably touching one another, and covered with strips when first put up. When they served as a shelter for us, however, the planks had shrunk.
>
> The roof was of shingles and did not leak. Along the comb an open space about a foot wide extended the entire length of the shed. The earth served as [a] floor, and the entrance was through a large barn door at each end.
>
> Along each side of this shelter, extending seven feet towards the center, were constructed four tiers of bunks, the lowest about one foot from the ground, the second three feet above this, the third three feet higher, while the fourth tier was on a level with the eaves.
>
> Upon these long shelves, not partitioned off, the prisoners slept, or lay down, heads to the wall, feet towards the center or passageway.[3]

Weather conditions during the winter of 1863-64 were especially severe in central Indiana. The new year of 1864 was ushered in with frigid temperatures that dipped to a bone-chilling twenty degrees below zero.

Along with the cold and icy conditions came a furious, swirling snowstorm that nearly buried the city of Indianapolis in white. It blocked streets and stopped railroad transportation north and south.

The cold and snow was unrelenting throughout January, and February brought little relief. The nasty conditions continued throughout March and even into April. The last snow to be recorded in local newspapers that season did not fall until April 16.[4]

"[There] were wide cracks, through which the winds whistled and the rain and snow beat in upon us," Wyeth said of Camp Morton's barracks. "I have often seen my top blanket white with snow when we hustled out for morning roll-call. About two feet of space was allotted to each man, making about 320 men housed in each shed. As we had no straw for bedding and as each man was allowed only one blanket, there was little comfort to be had in our

In this photo of Camp Morton, clothing is being dried on the line in front of drafty sheds that served as the Confederate prisoners' living quarters. Prisoners gather around the ditch that ran through the prison grounds. Photo from the Indiana Historical Society.

bunks until our miseries were forgotten in sleep. The scarcity of blankets forced us to huddle together, usually three in a group, with one blanket between us and the planks and the other two to cover us with."[5]

There were four stoves in the barracks, but Wyeth said only the strongest and most aggressive prisoners—Rebels ready and willing to fight their comrades for warmth—could get close enough to gain any benefit.

"To men, the greater number of whom had never been in a cold climate, the suffering was intense when with such surroundings the mercury was near zero," remembered Wyeth. "A number [of prisoners] were frozen to death and many more perished from disease brought on by exposure, added to their condition of emaciation from lack of food. I counted 18 bodies carried from the deadhouse one morning after an intensely cold night."

Though camp and Union military officials considered the food supply for the prisoners adequate, Wyeth characterized food rations during his incarceration as tremendously insufficient, especially in a community where foodstuffs were plentiful, even during the war. Not only did many Confederate soldiers go to bed hungry every night, some even died due to lack of nourishment in a land of plenty.

"I know from personal observation that many of my comrades died from starvation," wrote Wyeth. "Day after day it was easy to observe the progress of emaciation, until they became so weak that when attacked with an illness which a well-nourished man would easily have resisted and recovered from, they rapidly succumbed. The entire ration for one day was not enough for a single meal."[6]

The meat rations were often supplemented by soldiers harvesting the camp's rat population and any other unfortunate living creature—even dogs and cats—that happened to venture too close to the prisoner quarters. "One fat canine was captured by my messmates and was considered a feast," Wyeth recounted. "It was boiled and then baked and I was invited to the dinner. Although the scent of the cooking meat was tempting, I could not so far overcome my repugnance to this animal, as an article of diet, as to taste it. Those who ate it expressed themselves as delighted."[7]

While the mental imagery of malnourished young men relishing a meal of baked dog is troublesome enough, gradual starvation was not the most disturbing aspect of Wyeth's revelatory account in the national periodical. A pattern of cruel and blatant physical abuse—even cold-blooded murder—emerges from Wyeth's memories of a hellish Camp Morton environment. One prisoner, he recounted, was shot simply because he left the ranks after roll call was ended but before the official "break ranks" was commanded. The prisoner was freezing and he simply wanted to warm himself a moment at a fire a few feet away. "[The guard] did not even order the man back to the ranks," Wyeth remembered. "But calmly drew his pistol saying with profanity, 'I'll show you how to leave ranks before you are dismissed' and deliberately shot him."[8]

On many occasions, Wyeth saw prisoners brutally beaten with clubs simply because they would not move quickly out of the way of a guard or quit talking when a guard or officer passed by. For this type of offense, Wyeth once witnessed an officer grab a stick of firewood and bludgeon two prisoners in the head, leaving them lying on the ground unconscious.

Prisoners were regularly required, as punishment, to "mark time" in deep snow for more than an hour. Wyeth learned that one man lost both of his feet from gangrene as a result of this exposure and he later died.

Some sadistic guards, Wyeth wrote, derived special enjoyment from a "sport" that involved beating prisoners (with clubs fashioned from rolled-up heavy rubber cloths) as they trudged through the snow at night to the "sinks."

One night, two prisoners were on a detail that involved accompanying garbage wagons outside the prison walls. A guard accused them of trying to escape and shot them through the back, one in front of the other, with a single ball. Wyeth came to their aid. "I stayed by one of these men as he was dying and heard him solemnly assert, in the presence of death, that he had made no attempt to escape and that he and his comrade had been deliberately murdered."[9]

Another frequent evening activity practiced by some guards, wrote Wyeth, was firing shots into the prisoner barracks, for no logical reason other than sadism. In one such incident, Wyeth learned one morning that a prisoner in another barracks, a "Creole" from Louisiana, had been shot through the pelvis while sound asleep. The unfortunate young Louisianan, guiltless of any wrongdoing, later died of his wounds.[10]

When the men were not struggling to survive vicious attacks from prison guards, or wondering how long they could survive without proper nourishment, they were battling the creatures Wyeth called "vermin." "Crowded as we were, in close personal contact with all sorts and conditions of men, many of whom did not have a change of clothing, with no place to bathe except the open air, and this for months in a very cold atmosphere and with slim accommodations for boiling our apparel, it is not to be wondered at that all were infested with parasites. On a number of occasions, our committee forced those who were negligent in cleanliness to strip and boil their clothes, and would clip the hair from the heads of others who would not keep themselves clean of headlice."

While Wyeth and the other Camp Morton prisoners struggled with bitter daily realities of living amid squalor and being subjected to constant mental and physical abuse, all that they had to sustain themselves emotionally was a dream of someday going home. Wrote Wyeth, "With little to do, except to try to get something to eat, and keep from being eaten by vermin, the hours and days were necessarily long and weary. Men rarely talked of any subjects to the exclusion of a 'square meal' and the hope of an exchange, which meant—home."

The folks back home would not have a real picture of the horrors their beloved soldiers were subjected to at Camp Morton until after they were reunited. During the summer of 1862, Union officials had ordered that letters out of the camp would be limited to one page and contents could be only of a personal, private nature. From then on, censors eliminated graphic descriptions of prisoners' experiences in letters from Camp Morton.

This is quite apparent in a letter written from Camp Morton in June 1864 by Nathanial H. Ayres, of Hart County, Georgia, who served in the Second South Carolina Rifles as a private. Ayres wrote to his wife, Margaret:

> Dear wife. I seat myself in order to drop you a few lines informing you that I am well at present. I hope these lines may come through the lines and find you and the children all well and doing well. I have been in close confinement here seven long and lonely months. We had the coldest weather here last winter that I ever saw.

After a few more lines of a personal nature, he concluded, "I must close. I have written as much as they will allow me to write."[11]

Dr. John A. Wyeth finally made it home after he was released in February 1865, when the Civil War was drawing to a close. But an estimated two thousand young Confederate soldiers, many of them

Wyeth's prison comrades, would never leave Camp Morton. They would die there.

Far from Southern hearths and homes, these young men would be laid to rest under Indiana soil.

CHAPTER 7

A Stunned City and State React

Dr. John Wyeth had dropped a veritable bombshell on the city of Indianapolis and the entire the state of Indiana with his allegations in the April 1891 edition of *Century Monthly Magazine*. His charges of neglect and brutality at Camp Morton were "received with great indignation in the state of Indiana," wrote the authors of *Camp Morton 1861-1865.*[1] Soon after Wyeth's memories of his horrific experiences were made public to the nation, Indiana military and civic officials quickly organized to do "damage control." Too many reputations were on the line—many of them belonging to very wealthy and prominent citizens in the Hoosier state—to ignore his allegations.

The Department Encampment of the Grand Army of the Republic, a powerful Union veterans organization, had a meeting in Indianapolis on April 10, 1891, to formally "investigate" Wyeth's disturbing charges. The seven-member committee appointed by that group to look into Wyeth's charges had as its most prominent member Lew Wallace, the former Union officer, top military aide to Indiana's Civil War-era governor, Oliver P. Morton, and author of *Ben-Hur.*

Another prominent member of the GAR committee was James L. Mitchell. An attorney and former mayor of Indianapolis (during the 1870s), Mitchell had served as a Union major and had been involved in extensive combat.

W. R. Holloway, who had served as Governor Morton's private secretary during the Civil War, was selected by the committee to report the findings of its "investigation." The resulting report was submitted in full to *Century Monthly* and published in its September 1891 issue under the heading, "A Reply to 'Cold Cheer at Camp Morton.'" The GAR report accused Wyeth of grossly exaggerating conditions at the prison in some respects and of telling complete untruths in many other respects. The tone of the GAR report was generally sarcastic and condescending, often downright arrogant. It was altogether apparent that Dr. Wyeth's allegations had touched a major "nerve" and he had become a target for somewhat passionate retribution.

In the GAR report, Indiana military officials and civil leaders addressed each area of camp life that Wyeth had criticized and produced "witnesses" to dispute those charges. Holloway himself testified in the article that he found Dr. Wyeth's claims inconsistent with what he had personally witnessed at Camp Morton. He wrote:

> As a private secretary of Governor Morton, it was part of my duty to visit all of the camps and to learn something of their management. I talked with the prisoners in Camp Morton almost daily, visited their barracks, and ate of their food. I saw bread baked in the bakery. Save the new arrivals at Camp Morton, most of whom were ill and ragged, the prisoners were in good health and comfortably clothed.
>
> If [the prisoners] were hungry, cold or maltreated, they made no complaint to me, nor to anyone I ever heard. Any prison house will become irksome to those confined in it, although be it said that the prisoners at Camp Morton were made as comfortable as circumstances would permit.[2]

Holloway, in his personal testimony, articulated what would be a common theme in the GAR report: that the primary causes of death at Camp Morton were illnesses and malnutrition from which the Confederate soldiers were suffering prior to coming to the prison.

Holloway painted a much different portrait of the camp than Dr. Wyeth and other former prisoners who would later document their experiences in national publications. Holloway wrote:

> The most efficient causes of death in Camp Morton were the insufficient food and the exposure from which the rebel soldiers had suffered before they arrived at the prison. Ample hospital arrangements were made. Everything that kindness or humanity could suggest was done to alleviate the distressed condition of the prisoners.
>
> The prisoners themselves, very generally, were profuse in commendations of their treatment, and when the time cane for their exchange, many of them preferred to take the Oath of Allegiance, remaining North, than to be sent back to fight against the government that had manifested such kindness and magnanimity towards them.[3]

The GAR report contended that Dr. Wyeth's accusation that the camp's hospital facilities were "wholly inadequate" was unfounded. It argued that they were in fact equal to facilities used to house sick and injured Union soldiers during the war. Holloway quoted Dr. John M. Kitchen, who was "surgeon-in-chief" at the City Hospital (where the worst cases were sent from Camp Morton), as follows:

> Governor Morton ordered that there should be no distinction made between the Union soldiers and prisoners of war. All were treated alike; they had the same beds and bedding, clean underwear, nursing and medical care, medical aid, food, etc., etc.
>
> I have letters from ex-prisoners, written since the war, expressing their gratitude for kindness and attention shown them while under my care. I also remember that when prisoners were exchanged, their condition was better than that of the men who had guarded them.[4]

The officer in charge of hospital arrangements inside the prison camp, Col. Charles J. Kipp, pronounced the hospital there "a model one." His contentions were seconded by the camp commandant at the time, General Stevens (who was a colonel during the war). Stevens described Camp Morton's hospital facilities in glowing terms. "I gave the hospitals my personal attention. And they were run on the best possible plan. [They] had the reputation as being the cleanest in the country outside of Washington."[5]

Then came the issue of Dr. Wyeth's allegations that prisoners were insufficiently sheltered from the cold Indianapolis weather. His most disturbing charge on this topic was that many unprotected prisoners literally froze to death. Dr. Wyeth had written in his controversial article that he had personally "counted 18 bodies carried from the deadhouse one morning after an intensely cold night."[6]

This, contended the GAR report, was a complete fabrication. Holloway quoted Elijah Hedges, "now the oldest undertaker in the city" and an employee of the firm that buried prisoners at Camp Morton, as claiming: "There never were eighteen dead bodies in what was called the 'deadhouse' at one time."[7] Also quoted was Dr. J. W. Hervey, surgeon-in-charge of "Burnside Barracks," which were occupied by the Veteran Reserve Corps, the group that served as Camp Morton's prison guards. Said Hervey, "I remember the cold night, January 1, 1864. Our guards suffered fearfully, but no soldier or prisoner of war was frozen to death."[8]

Capt. Thomas Foster, who issued army rations to prisoners at

Camp Morton during the war, disputed Dr. Wyeth's allegations that
Confederate prisoners at Camp Morton were underfed. His contentions were quoted by Holloway in the GAR report from an adver-
tisement Foster had published in the April 8, 1891, edition of the
Nashville (Tenn.) Banner.

> I issued the usual army rations of provisions to both the National
> troops and Confederate prisoners. They are exactly alike. The rations
> to each were the same in quality and quantity. There were no differ-
> ences made between the prisoners and National troops in the field.
>
> The Camp Morton prisoners had even better fare. Instead of hard-
> tack, a well-equipped bakery on the spot furnished them soft and
> fresh baker's bread daily, my commissary depot supplying a prime arti-
> cle of flour for the consumption of the bakery.
>
> The best bacon and fresh beef were issued to the prisoners, and cof-
> fee, sugar, beans, hominy and rice . . . neither the troops nor the pris-
> oners could consume the liberal rations furnished by the government.
>
> It is within my knowledge that the winter quarters and bedding
> were about as good as were enjoyed by the National troops in the
> camp who guarded them, and who really suffered hardships from
> the winter severities when mounted as sentinels on the high platform
> near the top of the fence of the corral.
>
> Governor Morton was not the man to tolerate any but the most
> humane treatment of prisoners under his care and watchful eye, as
> were those of Camp Morton. It is true the prisoner's camp was not
> a paradise—it was not a parlor, nor were feather-beds issued to them
> by the Quartermaster's Department, but they were made comfort-
> able, had plenty to eat, pure water to drink and for washing, and
> were urged to keep themselves in good health by athletic sports
> and ball-playing.[9]

The most serious charges Dr. Wyeth made in his article in the
national magazine involved brutality he said his fellow prisoners
suffered at the hands of guards and other prison personnel.
Again, as with every other major accusation Dr. Wyeth leveled in
his article, the GAR report painted a much different portrait of
this aspect of prison life. Dr. Hervey contended that the only prisoners injured by guards and other prison personnel were those
who had it coming—whose actions merited severe physical retribution. Said Hervey, "Some of the prisoners were very insulting
to the officers and men over them. They would pelt the guards
with stones and broken bottles after night, several being severely

The grave marker of Gov. Oliver P. Morton, in Indianapolis's Crown Hill Cemetery. Photo by the author.

injured. The only prisoners that were ever shot were those who
attempted to escape and who did not stop when they were commanded to halt."[10]

Capt. James H. Rice, an officer in the reserve corps, also testified
in the GAR report that Camp Morton's Confederate prisoners were
not subjected to brutality.

> I was officer of the day every sixth day and a part of the time every
> fourth day. The statement that two prisoners were "brutally mur-
> dered" bears evidence of its untruthfulness on its face. I know of no
> case where prisoners were killed except in attempting to escape. I met
> with men who had been in Camp Morton as prisoners at Lexington,
> Kentucky, in 1866-67. The manner of their treatment was discussed
> and it was admitted that they had no just cause for complaint.

Surprisingly, the former camp commandant, Stevens, stopped
short of labeling Dr. Wyeth's accusation about brutality in the prison
a figment of the physician's imagination. In an offhanded way, he
seemed to be actually admitting that brutality did take place at the
prison while under his command. "There was no disposition on the
part of the officers to misuse the prisoners," he remarked. "There
were isolated cases of what might be looked upon as cruelty, but I
don't see how they could have happened, as Mr. Wyeth claims, without an investigation."

The last of all of the testimonials given in the GAR report came from
Gen. O. B. Wilcox, governor of the Soldiers' Home in Washington,
D.C. He was in command of the district that included Indianapolis
(though not the prison camp) during the summer and autumn of
1863. Wilcox's testimony paints another glowing portrait of camp life,
but it is curious that the GAR officials would close out their response to
Dr. Wyeth's charges with the Wilcox comments. The period Wilcox
described was before the timeframe that Dr. Wyeth identified as when
prison conditions began to severely deteriorate. Reported Wilcox:

> I have read the Wyeth article in "The Century" and I am sure
> no such state of things existed at Camp Morton while I was in com-
> mand of the district which included Indianapolis though not the
> prisoner's camp.
>   There were a number of trusties in the camp who were permitted
> to visit the city, and even attend the theater, in company with non-
> commissioned officers. Persons who were known to be loyal, or who
> presented letters from persons personally known to the officer in

charge of the camp, were permitted to visit the same at will.

Newsboys visited the camp regularly with the leading daily papers, and many of them did a good business in purchasing the rings made of cannel-coal, and breastpins made of bone, as well as small and curious articles carved out of wood by the prisoners, which they sold outside of camp, as relics.

The prisoners played baseball, and had good dramatic and glee clubs, and gave entertainments in the dining-room of the largest hospital. Amusements of all kinds were encouraged by the officers, and everything possible was done to make the prisoners contented.

Mr. Wyeth seems to have been particularly unfortunate in his army career, having been twice captured and compelled to spend most of the term of his enlistment in prison. This half-frozen, half-starved, emaciated youth . . . after his exchange was able to re-enter the Confederate army within a month and has lived to attempt a vicarious vindication of the horrors of Andersonville and other Southern prison-pens.[11]

Thus ended the GAR report. The defense had, in effect, rested its case. But Dr. Wyeth was not finished. His reputation and credibility had come under serious attack, and Dr. Wyeth had proven he was not a man who would meekly walk way from the hot fire of battle.

There would be more salvos fired at Camp Morton. And they were shots that would, once again, be heard around the world.

CHAPTER 8

"Walking Skeletons" and Missing Food

The Department Encampment of the Grand Army of the Republic had been given an opportunity to dispute Dr. John Wyeth's stunning charges in *Century Monthly Magazine,* and the organization apparently made the most of its opportunity. Dr. Wyeth, the GAR contended, was absolutely and categorically wrong. He was wrong about almost every aspect of prison life at Indiana's Camp Morton. The GAR report did not speculate about why Dr. Wyeth would want to fabricate such charges. It focused more on defending the prison and its staff than on attacking Dr. Wyeth (although it directed some sarcastic comments towards the physician).

Now, Dr. Wyeth would get another crack at Camp Morton. *Century Monthly Magazine* allowed him the opportunity to pen a "rejoinder" to the GAR report.

Dr. Wyeth was a prominent physician and medical researcher of his time, but he approached this task with the skill of a trained professional newspaper or magazine journalist. Wyeth did not simply rephrase and restate his contentions about Camp Morton. He brought in additional information to freshen his arguments and extensively quoted other former Camp Morton prisoners to support his own allegations. Wrote Wyeth, "Even the apologist of Camp Morton corroborates much of my narrative, and where he fails, my comrades, as it will be seen, made proof of its truthfulness positive and complete. These survivors, scattered over a vast territory without the possibility of collusion, give the one experience of hunger, cruelty, and suffering for lack of clothing and proper protection from the rigors of the Northern winter."[1]

In the aftermath of Dr. Wyeth's first article in *Century Monthly Magazine,* a flood of articles and letters was published in newspapers and periodicals across the nation. In his rejoinder, Wyeth quoted one of them—an editorial in the April 6, 1891, edition of the Buffalo Courier. "Painful as it is to admit," wrote the unnamed author of the editorial, "the presumption is in favor of the truth of [Dr. Wyeth's] narrative. The Ration for which the Government contracted and paid was sufficient and all that military prisoners had a reasonable right to expect, but, as Dr. Wyeth asserts for Camp Morton and Mr. Carpenter for Johnson's Island [a Union prison on Lake Erie], the prisoners did not get it. And there was never a class of men who could be robbed with more impunity. Enemies in a strange land, their protests were easily suppressed."[2]

The *Buffalo Courier* raised an issue that Dr. Wyeth explored further in his rejoinder. This was the serious allegation of thievery from government stores of food rations that were supposed to feed Confederate prisoners. Wyeth quoted P. M. Gapen, a grocer in Indianapolis, as follows:

> During the early winter of 1864, the grocery firm of P. M. Gapen and Co. of this city, of which I was a senior member, purchased through parties now deceased, twenty bags of coffee at twenty-one cents, twenty barrels of sugar, ten barrels of rice, and not less than forty boxes of candles at correspondingly low figures.
>
> Later, large quantities were offered my firm at similar reductions from current wholesale prices. I then inquired where those goods came from, and was informed that they came from, or were supplied for, the prisoners at Camp Morton, and declined further offerings.[3]

The author of this book has found no evidence that Indianapolis officials investigated this charge, possibly because it would have been hard to track down the guilty party or parties more than a quarter-century after the alleged thievery had taken place.

Dr. Wyeth also took aim, from his own experience and testimonies of other prisoners, at the GAR committee's contention that no prisoners were murdered at Camp Morton. "I myself saw the pistol fire and the man fall," he wrote in his rejoinder. "And, I have the testimony of more than a dozen men who also saw this monster [a guard whose last name was Baker] do this crime, and yet it was concealed. I have the proof that he shot a second prisoner after this, yet the commanding officer [contended] he had never heard of either case."[4]

The following are portions of some testimonies published in Dr.

Wyeth's rejoinder from men who corroborated his version of conditions at Camp Morton.

C. B. Kilgore, a congressman from Texas, stated, "I was a prisoner of war at Camp Morton for a few weeks in the winter of 1863-64. You have drawn a very moderate picture of the horrors of that horrible pen."[5]

S. Pasco, a U.S. senator from Florida, stated:

> I was sent to Camp Morton in May, 1864. This building [where he was housed] was little more than a shed. Some of the incidents of cruel and inhuman conduct which you mentioned occurred before my residence there, but were among the current traditions of the camp. I was a prisoner in all seventeen months, and no clothing was ever issued to me. Scanty food, harsh and brutal treatment and insufficient shelter during the winter months were doubtless the cause . . . of the large percentage of deaths during the ten months of my confinement in the camp.[6]

Dr. W. P. Parr, acting assistant surgeon, United States Army, stated:

> I was assigned to duty at Camp Morton February 12, 1864, and served till March, 1865, when I resigned.
>
> Your picture of the suffering of the prisoners falls short of the horrid reality. My blood gets hot, even at this remote day, when I recall those scenes of cruelty and cowardly brutality. [The prisoners] did freeze; how many I do not remember, but I do know that a great many of the frozen dead bodies were carried from their bunks to the dead-house, where many others died soon after they were brought into the hospital.
>
> I felt then, as I do now, that it was a lasting shame upon our country that human beings, prisoners of war, should be thus forced to occupy a position where they must freeze to death, while ample means to prevent it were close at hand.[7]

C. S. S. Baron, owner of the Baron Manufacturing Company of Bellaire, Ohio, stated:

> I read your article in *The Century* to my wife, and it so closely resembled what I have been telling her for years that she declared you and I must have been messmates. During the period when the men were being vaccinated I saw a big brutal sergeant knock a prisoner down, place his knee on the man's chest, and present his revolver at him, because he protested against being vaccinated.
>
> In 1864, one very cold night a prisoner of our barracks, who was in ill health, went to the stove to warm. He was discovered by the

guard, who came up to him saying, "I'll warm you" and with this expression shot [the prisoner]. The poor fellow rolled off the box he was sitting upon. I do not think he even groaned.

I think the two men you mention as being fatally shot through from behind were the two from my mess who met with that fate. They were detailed one morning for work outside the prison. They were brought in about noon and taken . . . to a hospital tent, where some hours later they died.

Knowing they were mortally wounded, they said that one of the guards made a threat to kill a rebel because a relative of his had been killed at the front by the rebels. Being alarmed, they were afraid that this man would do them harm, who however assured them there was no danger. The guard, awaiting his opportunity, got them in line and fired a ball through both.

The infernal mania for shooting into the barracks at night I could not understand. If the good people in this country could have been convinced of the truth of one half of the tyranny, starvation, cruelty and murder going on inside that fence, they would in the righteous wrath have leveled the whole thing to the ground, and probably would have visited lynch law upon those who were concerned in this great wrong.[8]

Dr. J. L. Rainey, a practicing physician in Henry County, Tennessee, stated:

The attempt to refute your narrative, *Cold Cheer Camp Morton* will be utterly futile. There are yet living hundreds of men who know that your statement falls short in details of many cruelties inflicted upon prisoners there by soldiers and officers, and many privations which were maliciously inflicted.

As an individual I had little cause to complain (as I was made dispensing clerk in the hospital), but I am bound in honor to say that no man can prove that there is a shadow of falsehood in your statement. I was in the presence of the two men who were shot from behind and mortally wounded with the single ball, and heard the statement made by one of them that they were murdered.

George Douglass, of Columbia, Tennessee, member of my company, who was nearly blind, was taken out on detail and shot. I examined the body at the dead-house. He was shot in the back and it was murder.[9]

Dr. W. E. Shelton, a practicing physician in Austin, Texas, stated, "I was confined at Camp Morton about June 1, 1863. In July or August, I was assigned to duty as physician to the sick in quarters.

During one very cold spell, several prisoners froze to death and many others died from the effects of cold. I have read *Cold Cheer* at *Camp Morton* and I am prepared to swear that it is true."[10]

The Rev. W. S. Wightman, pastor of the Southern Methodist Church in Bennettsville, South Carolina, stated, "How I managed to stand the starvation and cold of that awful prison is something wonderful to me. My emaciation when I reached home was so great that my family scarcely recognized me. I can substantiate what you say in your article—the harsh treatment, the brutality, the horrible meanness. I am witness to the fact that many a poor fellow perished from cold and starvation."[11]

The Rev. W. H. Groves, a Presbyterian pastor in Lynnville, Tennessee, stated, "Dr. Wyeth graphically and truthfully describes Camp Morton. To strike a match to look at a sick or dying comrade was to be shot by guards. Our rations were so meager that men became walking skeletons. My feet were so frozen that I suffered intensely and could not wear my shoes for over a year."[12]

The Rev. Samuel Tucker, pastor of the Cumberland Presbyterian Church, Springfield, Arkansas, stated:

> I can fully corroborate your statements concerning the treatment of prisoners. There were fifty-one men in our squad I arrived with and thirty-two of these perished there. I have seen the prisoners struggling with each other to devour the dirty matter thrown out of the hospital's kitchen. Rats were eaten, and I have seen dog-meat peddled out by the prisoners. The murdering of prisoners, clubbing, tying them up by the thumbs was known to all there. I could put the entire piece of meat given me for a day's allowance in my mouth at one time.[13]

Dr. Wyeth's rejoinder to the GAR report put the prominent physician and medical researcher back on the offensive. Other Confederate veterans and former prisoners of the Indianapolis camp were ready to dip pen in ink to record their memories and, like Dr. Wyeth, to have those memories published in the national news media.

CHAPTER 9

"A Demon in Human Flesh"

"That den of misery a little north of Indianapolis known as Camp Morton"—this was how J. K. Womack, a Baptist pastor from North Carolina, described the Civil War prison camp.[1] He was one of scores of Confederate veterans and ex-prisoners at Camp Morton who would publicly dispute the Department Encampment of the Grand Army of the Republic's official report about the prison. Womack's support of Dr. John A. Wyeth's complaints about Camp Morton was published in the December 1898 issue of *Confederate Veteran* magazine.

"There was not a bunk in the division, so our bed during the winter [of 1863] was an oilcloth spread upon the earth in the aisle of these barracks," wrote Womack. "Those who had preceded us were in much want. They were dirty, pale, emaciated, ragged and lousy. Only a few had a change of clothing. We slept in our clothing every night to keep from freezing."[2]

Serving in the Confederate Army had been no picnic for Womack, who often had to go hungry and unsheltered when he was preparing for battle. But the difficult life of a Rebel during the Civil War could not match Womack's experiences as a prisoner at Camp Morton.

> Camp life as a Confederate soldier was hard, but prison life in Camp Morton was harder. Daily rations were eaten almost immediately upon being issued. We were supplied with one loaf of bread and one small piece of beef, and nothing more. [Often] we became so hungry that we would stand and look for the wagons to come through the gates with our bread.
>
> The Yankee sergeant who called the roll for our division was named Fiffer [Pfeifer]. He was . . . really a demon in human flesh. I have seen him walk through our barracks with a heavy stick in his

79

hand, striking right and left to the heads and faces, backs or stomachs of the poor starving prisoners, as though they were so many reptiles crying out: "This is the way you whip your Negroes." I dislike to write this, but it ought to go down in history.[3]

Womack had also witnessed the work of one Sergeant Baker, whom other former prisoners, including Dr. Wyeth, cited as being especially violent.

> One bitter cold morning while we were standing in line stamping the Earth to keep from freezing, a pistol shot was heard, and immediately the piteous cries of a prisoner wafted to our ears. The poor fellow had stepped a little out of line at roll call, and for this "crime" was shot down [by Sergeant Baker].
>
> We existed . . . with the thermometer below zero, in open stables without door shutters, hungry and shivering with cold, having only one stove for two hundred and fifty men. How good a piece of corn bread from home would have been at that time!
>
> While memory lasts I can never forget the great war and that cruel prison.[4]

John Franklin Champenois, who had served a term as mayor of Shubuta, Mississippi, would also likely never forget his experiences as a prisoner at Camp Morton. He wrote about his time there soon after Dr. Wyeth's articles appeared. The Champenois piece is identified as having appeared in a publication only known as *The Standard.* He wrote:

> Reading from [*Century Monthly Magazine*] of April 1, I find an interesting and truthful sketch of life in Camp Morton from the pen of Dr. John A. Wyeth, now of New York, which forcibly reminds of life at Camp Morton as I saw it.
>
> Much has been said and written of the horrors of prison life in Camps Andersonville and Libby. Life in either was no doubt bad, but those of us who sojourned at Camp Morton did not dwell in paradise, as I will attempt to show.[5]

Corroborating assertions from Dr. Wyeth and others that prisoners did not receive food rations that were allocated them from the U.S. government, Champenois wrote the following:

> The government may have allowed the rations, but no such

quantity per man was ever issued at Camp Morton. The U.S. contractor very likely could tell why the difference. What they did issue, we were too hungry to take time to weigh. That it was fearfully short of our wants, I know. That a good sized, healthy house cat would have eaten a twenty-four hours ration, been hungry, and as we did, howled for more, I also know.[6]

Champenois, who was a prisoner from 1863 to 1865, was all too familiar with the cruelty exhibited by some guards at Camp Morton.

There was a federal officer connected with the prison whom we called "Bloody Hell." On clear, cold days, a number of the weak, sick and emaciated would gather in the rear of the cook house where they could enjoy the sunshine and flavor of the food rising from the steaming cookpots. Often I have seen "Bloody Hell" steal on his unsuspecting victims with bludgeon in hand and whack! whack! over the head and shoulders would be the first notice of his presence. Why, it's bliss to hate the scoundrel twenty-five years after the war.

Only three at a time were permitted at the sinks. I recall that once on a clear night, a prisoner, after giving the usual signal, was shot and killed in cold blood, without warning. No excuse was rendered, only that too many were at the sinks.

It was currently reported that this man was killed by Baker, who was cruelty personified. At night, when the poor, sick, freezing prisoners would disobey orders and leave their bunks to gather around the stove to get a little warmth from the dying embers, then this man, Baker, would come to the door and empty his revolver down the warm passage way, with this yell: "Rats to your holes." It was to be shot or freeze and the one had more terrors than the other.

Baker occasionally winged his man. However, he was too mean to live and the devil called his own, at which no prisoner went in mourning.[7]

In 1912, two brothers from Alabama, Mitchell B. and William Robert Houghton, documented their experiences in the Confederate Army in the book *Two Boys in the Civil War and After.* They joined the Confederacy in 1861. William, an eighteen-year-old schoolteacher at the time, joined the Second Georgia Infantry. He fought in major battles and was wounded several times. William was paroled on April 12, 1865, at Appomattox Court House, Virginia.

Mitchell was only sixteen when he joined the Fiftieth Alabama. He had been wounded twice in combat and was captured by Union forces in the foothills of Lookout Mountain a few days after the Battle of Chickamauga.

In *Two Boys in the Civil War and After,* the authors spoke specifically about Dr. Wyeth's campaign to bring to light the horrors of Camp Morton, writing, "Dr. John A. Wyeth, an eminent physician now of New York, who was a prisoner also in Camp Morton, wrote a series of articles on prison life in Camp Morton which were published in the *Century Magazine.* The story of the abuse, cruelty, graft, neglect, starvation and mortality connected with the conduct and management of that prison makes the history of Andersonville mild in comparison when the resources of the two governments are considered."[8]

In using the term *graft,* Mitchell Houghton, who came to Camp Morton as a prisoner in September 1863, was no doubt addressing the widespread contention that food rations intended for prisoners were stolen and sold. He wrote:

> Our bread was cooked in a bakery outside the walls and was good and wholesome but only a half pound loaf was allowed daily. The daily allowance was devoured in a few minutes. Our meats were cooked in big cauldrons inside the camp and was usually beef. The general ration was cut down to less than half the army allowance and many men slowly starved to death.
>
> Slow starvation among a lot of idle men gradually robs them of every noble instinct and transforms them into weak but ravenous beasts. It was curious but tragic to hear the prisoners recount the story daily and hourly of former feasts and revive the memory of every ample dinner they had enjoyed in the past.
>
> With glowing eyes and animated faces they delighted to tell of the good things provided by their wives and mothers in the halcyon days in Dixie. The subject [food] became a passion—a frenzy, and men only existed to remember what had been.
>
> There was a small ditch or canal across the grounds through which flowed a small sluggish stream that was always more or less filthy. Thousands of cray fish or craw fish as we would wont to call them bred in the stream and the men would gather them for the purpose of making soup. Every dog, cat and rat also had to run for his life for the hungry men were omnivorous.
>
> The mortality among the prisoners was frightful. Insufficient food, and clothing, no bedding, little medical attention and the dull

hopeless existence of prison life in a severe climate sapped the remaining vitality of the men and they died by the score.[9]

Houghton joined many other former prisoners in speaking out about cruel guards and officers at Camp Morton. He wrote:

> Some of the officers commanding were cruel and tyrannical and inflicted all sorts of punishment on many of the men who committed thoughtless acts or were in any way refractory.
>
> Often men were reported by spies and traitors among us to the commander for the expression of any sentiment of hope for victory for our side or criticism of the Federal conduct of the war or the management of the prison. Tying up by the hands, bucking and gagging were common.
>
> Whenever a prisoner escaped they seemed to take revenge on many of the men by more than usual severity of treatment. It was not uncommon for a guard to shoot a prisoner for very slight infraction of the rules, and one little officer said to have been from Missouri delighted to show his authority by abusing the men in every conceivable manner.[10]

In his articles in *Century Monthly Magazine,* Dr. Wyeth had written that many Confederate prisoners had literally frozen to death during unusually cold winter months at Camp Morton. This contention was hotly disputed by the GAR report. But Houghton, like Dr. Wyeth, gave a firsthand account of this tragic occurrence.

> With two other men I had the top bunk at the North end on the East side of one of the barracks. The passage way between the two houses was covered but had a ground floor. The gabled end was not entirely closed up and the cold northwest wind was very severe. We had an old rubber blanket to spread on our rough plank bed and two other thin hair blankets for cover.
>
> We took turns as to sleeping in the middle for that was the warmest position. The winter was a very cold one, snow covering the ground more than forty days in succession, with two or more blizzards intervening.
>
> On one of these cold nights we laid down to try to sleep. One of my companions named Searcy, from Eufaula, Alabama, occupied the middle while I was on the outside most exposed. Searcy was over medium sized, well proportioned and seemed strong and vigorous.

During the latter part of the night he talked of his adventures in battle, describing how he had shot three men in a certain fight, declaring that he knew he had killed them, and detailing all the circumstances. He expressed regret that he had not slain more, and bitterly upbraided the enemy for the treatment he was receiving, denouncing them in the strongest and most vigorous terms of which he was capable.

He talked on while we his two bedfellows, were partially benumbed with cold and semi-conscious from drowsiness. He finally became quiet and when the morning came we found him dead.[11]

Like so many of his Confederate comrades, Houghton was desperate enough facing such woeful conditions inside the prison that he was willing to risk life and limb to try to escape from it. He told of how prisoners often attempted to escape the prison and of his own unsuccessful effort.

Tunneling was a favorite method of attempting to escape from the prison. The black soil of the prison enclosure was about three feet deep and underneath was a thick stratum of white sand. The men would commence under their bunks and dig with knives, sticks or any tool they could improvise down to the sand and then scrape out a tunnel toward the guard wall.

The dirt was carried away in their pockets or they would tie a string around the bottom of the legs of their pants and partially fill the space around their limbs with the sand, then walk out and slowly scatter it about on the grounds so as not to attract attention.

They often patiently worked for weeks until they estimated they had run their shaft outside the guard wall, usually about fifty yards, and await a dark night to open out on the outside. A number of men escaped in this way, but spies and traitors made it dangerous and nearly every effort made during the last six months of our confinement was defeated by some scoundrel who would betray the workers.

In one or more instances the guards would allow the prisoner to open the outside end of the tunnel and shoot him down as he emerged. A preconcerted movement was projected for a general escape. It was one of those unaccountable uprisings that take possession of men without a head or immediate cause. No one appeared to direct but it was whispered from man to man and caused great suppressed excitement. For some reason it was reported that most of the guard for the prison had been withdrawn leaving barely sufficient men to mount the guard on the walls.

It was believed that the Confederates were threatening some

nearby point and all their men were needed to repel them. On a certain night armed with rocks and sticks, we were, about eight o'clock to scale the east wall, rush the guard and escape to the country. Hundreds of us drifted in the direction indicated. We were desperate and did not take into account the risk. I had several stones of convenient size to knock a guard down if he offered resistance.

The few sentinels could not kill all of the mob and we could get over before others could come to the rescue. Then the sentinels on the walk high up on the walls would not be able to shoot often or accurately with hundreds of stones being hurled at them. We were in striking distance when we heard the bugle calls on the outside, the double quick of infantry, the unlimbering of artillery and the tramp of cavalry. We had been betrayed and sullenly returned to our quarters.[12]

Not long after this harrowing episode, Houghton would finally taste freedom again. In late 1864, he was released from Camp Morton as part of a prisoner exchange. Houghton, and the other fortunate comrades who were a part of this exchange, boarded freight cars in Indianapolis and embarked on a long, slow journey back into Confederate country and eventually to Richmond, Virginia.

It was a ragged, emaciated lot of men, spiritless and weak from long confinement and ill treatment that once more entered Dixie. Our heroic fellow soldiers guarding the lines, looked on us with tender compassion for they were in dire straits themselves and the coming collapse of Confederate hopes cast a baleful shadow over the remnant of [Robert E.] Lee's once invincible army.

They appeared to us as men who realized that their fate was fixed but who were determined to meet the consequences without an exhibition of fear. We went into camp for a time but whether for a want of equipment or in compliance with terms of release we were dismissed subject to call. The order for again entering ranks never came, for communications were cut off from all directions and the end of all things hoped for by the Confederates was at hand.[13]

Another former prisoner who came to Dr. Wyeth's defense was Dr. Thomas E. Spotswood of Fairford, Alabama, grandson of Revolutionary War general Alexander Spotswood. His experiences at Camp Morton were documented in the *Memphis Commercial* newspaper (no date of publication is available).

Spotswood was a private in Company F, Fifty-Third Alabama Cavalry, when he was captured at the Battle of Resaca, Georgia, on May 15, 1864. He arrived in Indianapolis on May 22. During the first three months of his incarceration in Camp Morton, Spotswood said 25 percent of his comrades (from the forty men who were captured along with him) died of various prison diseases.

Not long after his arrival in Camp Morton, Spotswood was introduced to the cruel behavior of the infamous Sergeant Baker and other violent guards. He wrote:

> Soon after our arrival we made the acquaintance of one Sergeant Baker, who, we learned, had the reputation of having shot a prisoner, and who seemed to us to be looking out for a chance to try his hand again. Soon another poor fellow was added to his list, and shortly after he himself was missing, and the report reached us that he was dying—then that he was dead.
>
> A worthy companion of Sergeant Baker, John Pfeifer, a fine looking young man, was put in charge. The first dastardly act of his that I saw was in the early fall of '64, when, with an axe-handle, he beat and knocked down six men for some trifling disobedience of orders. Three of them with arms broken and two with heads badly damaged went to the hospital for treatment.
>
> During the winter, when the thermometer was below zero, I saw this fiend strip a man and give him a bath in a tub of water, using a common broom to scrub him with, and this fiendish deed was repeated the second time. I heard that both men died, though I do not know it of my own knowledge. I saw the baths given.
>
> I saw this man shoot a prisoner under my bunk for being up after bed-time. The poor fellow was one of the improvement kind; had sold his blanket and coat and was trying to keep warm over a few coals in the stove, when Pfeifer came suddenly to the door of the barracks; the prisoner ran under the lower bunk of my bed, and, failing to respond promptly to the order to come out, was fired on, the shell entering his heel and coming out near the knee. This bullet, no doubt, saved his life, as he was sent to the hospital, where he received kind treatment. Without blankets he could not have survived the winter of '64 and '65.

Spotswood also substantiated other ex-prisoners' stories of abuse and neglect during the coldest winter months in Indianapolis.

> This brings me to that dreadful month of January, 1865, when we suffered most from the terrible cold. We were unable to remain outside but a few moments, as our clothing and shoes were thin and in

rags, so were forced to trot round in circles on the mud floors of our pens, made soft by the snow brought in on the feet of the men. These trotting circles of men would last all day, new men taking the place of those dropping out from exhaustion.

It was during this terrible weather we would be forced to remain in line at roll-call for two hours at a time, because some sergeant had miscounted his men, or some poor fellow would be found dead in his bunk and was overlooked. Many men were frozen in this way and were carried to the hospital, where but few recovered, though when once in the hands of the kind doctors and nurses they were sure of good attention and warm clothing.

Men died constantly, seemingly without a cause. They would appear less cheerful and less interested in life, and next morning, when summoned to roll-call, would be found dead, either from star-vation or cold, God only knows which. Many went this way and many to the hospital never to return.

During this terrible month our guards were changed, and the new-comers must needs practice on the poor prisoners, some of them practically dying, to see if they could not add to sufferings already too great to be borne.

One might I saw through a crack in the stable eight or ten men being drilled in the snow with a shoe in each hand, this being for the amusement of the new guard and for punishment to the prisoners for talking after going to bed.

These are some of the indignities that can be put into print, but there were things more cruel and revolting perpetrated by these guards on the defenseless men that cannot be printed. If these numerous instances of shameful cruelty came under my personal observation, what number must have been perpetrated that none are living to record?

The outrages practiced by the guards and sergeants were not all we were subjected to in December, 1864. There was an order issued by the commanding officer that the men should not remain in barracks (after the doctor has passed through) from 9 o'clock A.M. until 3 o'clock. Poorly clad, starving men were compelled to stand around in the snow until hundreds had their feet so badly frost-bitten that their toes came off.

This cruel order was persisted in till many men died from expo-sure, when the order was countermanded. The excuse given for the order was that the men stayed in doors too much and would be ben-efited by exercise. Great Heavens!

Had these officers raised the ragged coat or blanket from the first figure they met and looked at the emaciated, itch-scarred, vermin-eaten creature, they would have seen that the men needed more food and warm clothing to hold life in them, instead of more snow and cold north wind. I am told that the people of Indianapolis deny that these terrible things occurred in their fair city.[14]

Like Dr. Wyeth and many other former Camp Morton prisoners, Spotswood believed that poor treatment of Confederate prisoners during the Civil War had been largely ignored and denied by citizens of Indiana and other Northern states. "I agree with you, sir, that the cruelties suffered by the prisoners of both armies should not have been laid before the public," he wrote. "But since our friends on the other side have done so much to show how cruel the South was, and still continue to publish these sad and horrible facts, and even move the prison buildings to northern cities to keep these facts fresh in the minds of each succeeding generation, it is but fair that we of the South should let the world know that the prison pens of the North were no whit better than the worst in the South."[15]

Interestingly, many years prior to these and Dr. Wyeth's revelations, another former Confederate prisoner at Camp Morton had taken an opportunity to inform readers of one of the nation's largest publications about conditions in the prison. In a letter to the editor of the *New York Times* penned in June 1867, J. G. Wilson, president of Huntsville Female College, wrote of his experience at the camp during six months in the fall and winter of 1863-64.

> Many rebel prisoners . . . spent that winter [of 1863-64] without a blanket, and the scant and ragged summer clothing worn when captured. Scores of the men in dead of winter slept in [old former cattle sheds], upon the bare ground without covering, huddling together like hogs to keep from freezing.
>
> It is well known to hundreds now living that several died, actually frozen to death, while large numbers were so badly frostbitten as to be lamed for life. Men barely able to crawl through weariness from insufficient food and disease consequence upon exposure, were forced, in the severest winter weather, to stand for roll call for two and often three or more hours in line, like soldiers on dress parade, and cursed like brutes or beaten over the head with sabres or clubs, and sometimes shot for moving a little to keep from freezing.
>
> A quiet, orderly man, an Englishman named Coats, belonging to my division, was murdered in cold blood by a private of the Invalid Corps named Baker, who was a guard. Instead of being tried and punished, Baker, though a private, was sent next morning to take

charge, as Sergeant, of our division, in which position he heaped upon the defenseless men every indignity that so inhuman a wretch could devise.

The above, and the half has not been told are plain, unexaggerated facts, which can be substantiated by most unquestionable testimony, and for the truth of which I pledge my character and reputation as a minister of the gospel.[16]

CHAPTER 10

Camp Morton's Final Days

By April 1, 1865, only 1,408 prisoners remained at Camp Morton. Military and civic officials began to plan how best to release the Confederate prisoners—now Confederate veterans—so that they could return to their families, friends, and what was left of their homelands.

Preference was given to those who had refused exchange and indicated their willingness to take the oath of allegiance. Camp officials administered the oath to these men, and they were discharged and furnished with transportation home.

By early June 1865, the camp was nearly empty. Only 308 prisoners were left there. Many of the ragged and penniless Confederate veterans applied for work as soon as they were released. But most headed south, for home. A reporter wrote in the *Indianapolis Journal* on June 14, 1865:

> Yesterday . . . the last remnant of the rebel prisoners confined in Camp Morton were released.
>
> In tattered grey and butternut the poor fellows straggled down our streets in search of transportation to their homes. The departure of many of these has been delayed because they were in the hospital.
>
> As we saw them, haggard and pale, tottering along with their little poverty-stricken bundles, we felt sincerely sorry for them. In our heart there was no bitterness of feeling against them: and we were glad, without qualification, that they were free once more. . . .
>
> They go back to conquered country—to overgrown fields, to ruined villages, to homes, the chimneys of which are left. This could not be helped. War is a hard thing and it leaves a black and damning trail.[1]

Among the last of the prisoners to leave Camp Morton were forty members of the Veteran Reserve Corps who had been consigned to the guardhouse for mutiny. They were given a dishonorable discharge without pay and released.[2]

When the Camp Morton Confederate prisoners returned home, they had plenty of horror stories to tell friends and family about their experiences "up North." A letter sent from Camp Morton during the cold Indianapolis winter of 1865 by Henry Hays Forwood, a Confederate soldier from Gosport, Alabama, revealed his anxiety about making it home safely. "For fear this may be the last opportunity I will have to write you," he wrote to his brother, "I will bid you all farewell."

But Forwood did survive and was able to return to his family in Alabama. Shortly after he had regained his freedom, he wrote a letter to his brother that no Union prison camp official would be able to censor.

> While I was in [Camp Morton], I was starving most of my time. I have went many a day without eating but one meal a day. We were treated very rough [by] the commander of the prison and Fifer [Pfeifer], a dutchman who used to come in the prison and beat the prisoners with large sticks just for the fun of the thing.
>
> They shot six times at me while in the bull pen as the boys called it and there was plenty other things they done in that place too numerous to mention.[3]

Ex-Rebels who had been held captive in other Northern war prisons had similar stories to tell. In Illinois's Alton Prison, hundreds of Confederate prisoners suffered from the effects of scurvy, even though Alton was a major produce center in the Midwest. According to accounts, with bloody and diseased gums and their teeth falling out, ailing Reb prisoners would peer out over the thirty-foot-high prison walls and onto the neighboring hilltops, which were covered with pear, peach, and crabapple trees. Prisoners literally begged the guards for some of the trees' life-saving nutrition, but they were cruelly denied the fruit.

At the New York prison Elmira (called "Hellmira" by Confederate prisoners), the chief surgeon, E. L. Sanger, was said to have boasted that he had "killed more Rebs than any soldier at the front." Sanger resigned his post in order to avoid court martial for his criminal treatment of sick and vulnerable Confederate prisoners.

Intoxicated guards at Camp Douglas in Chicago frequently inflicted arbitrary punishments upon blameless Southern prisoners.

Once, when a guard accidentally slipped and fell, a North Carolinian who could not contain his laughter was shot and killed on the spot. Other prisoners there were made to pull their pants down and sit with nothing under them on snow and frozen ground for the crime of "spitting too much."

Confederate prisoners at Camp Douglas were frequently forced to ride the infamous so-called "Morgan's Mule," which was a twelve-foot-high carpenter's sawhorse. With weights attached to prisoners' legs, the sharpened top plank would tear through their flesh, leaving the men unable to walk for days.

Unfortunately, "Morgan's Mule" was a particular favorite of tourists, who paid to climb the observation tower and gaze out at the prisoners. On days when no punishment was scheduled, innocent prisoners were forced to ride the "Mule" solely for the entertainment of the paying tourists.

Even the *New York Daily News* spoke out about conditions at the Rock Island Prison in Illinois. It described daily rations as consisting of one-third of a pound of bread and a "two-inch square of meat supplemented when possible by dogs, rats and mice."

Guards at Camp Chase in Columbus, Ohio, were said to take great pleasure in watching starving Confederates battle each other for apple cores and melon rinds that they threw onto the prison's paths. Prisoners there were also often hanged by their toes or forced to stand barefoot in the snow. The bodies of many dead Confederate prisoners at Camp Chase were sold to a medical school in Cleveland, Ohio.

Bodies of prisoners who died in Camp Morton were not sold to a medical school, but neither were they treated with the respect and honor generally accorded to soldiers who die during a time of war.

Confederates who died there were buried at Greenlawn Cemetery, near downtown Indianapolis. Some of the bodies were later exhumed and returned to relatives in the South. In the late 1860s, Greenlawn ceased to be used as a public burial place, and industrial developments began to encroach upon the site.

Officers of Confederate veterans' organizations occasionally inquired as to the condition of the graves of the Confederates who died at Camp Morton, but nothing was done about permanently memorializing them or improving their condition.[4]

In the 1870s, the Vandalia Railroad, needing part of the ground for an engine house and additional tracks, exchanged some property on the west side of the cemetery for ground on the North Line, where there were two rows of graves. The bodies from those two rows were removed and reburied in two parallel trenches, but the new graves were not marked.

In 1906, Col. William Elliott, detailed by the War Department to locate the burial places of the Confederate dead, examined the area and decided that a plot about forty feet wide by two hundred feet long was where the re-interments had been made in the 1870s. This space was enclosed by an iron fence. In 1912, the federal government finally erected a monument there in honor of the Confederate prisoners buried at Greenlawn Cemetery.[5]

With growing industry in the area pressing hard upon the memorial, the Southern Club of Indianapolis asked the Board of Park Commissioners for permission to remove the monument to Garfield Park, located on the south side of Indianapolis. In 1928, the move was made. In 1931, the War Department exhumed the Confederate remains from Greenlawn and moved them to the northwest corner of Crown Hill Cemetery, which is often referred to as the "Confederate Mound."

This monument was placed in 1928 at Garfield Park on the south side of Indianapolis to honor Confederate soldiers who died at Camp Morton. Photo by the author.

A new marker at Crown Hill Cemetery memorialized "1,616 Unknown Confederates." But records were subsequently discovered that revealed all of the names, dates of death, and ranks of the deceased prisoners. So, civic leaders in Indianapolis created "The Crown Hill Cemetery Project" to give the veterans proper recognition.

During a lavish ceremony in 1993 in which the dead Confederate veterans were finally accorded the respect and dignity they deserved, a new Confederate Memorial was dedicated. Hundreds of onlookers were on hand to honor the Confederate veterans, including community leaders, military leaders, and former U.S. representative Andy Jacobs, a supporter of the project. Also taking part in the ceremony were military honor guards from the U.S. Army and Civil War reenactors.

Crown Hill Cemetery has been listed on the National Register of Historic Places since 1973. More than twenty-five thousand people pass through the site annually, many on special occasions such as Memorial Day, Benjamin Harrison's birthday (Harrison, former U.S.

Remains of Confederate soldiers who died at Camp Morton are buried here at Crown Hill Cemetery in Indianapolis. Inscribed monuments on the ground show the names and other important information about the dead. Photo by the author.

This dignified marker is located at the "Confederate Mound" at Crown Hill Cemetery in Indianapolis, behind the large markers on the ground that list identities of Confederate soldiers who died at Camp Morton. Photo by the author.

president, was an Indianapolis native), Veteran's Day, and a fall Victorian Day celebration.

Each year on Memorial Day, numerous Civil War reenactment units honor the Camp Morton soldiers in a special ceremony conducted in front of the Confederate Mound. The ceremony includes several rifle and cannon salutes.

Crown Hill sells a book called *Confederate Burials in Crown Hill Cemetery, Marion County*. It details some of the history of Camp Morton, along with the first and last name of each soldier interred there, his rank, military unit, date of death, and state where he lived.

What became of Camp Morton after the Civil War? Disposal of its property began soon after the prisoners left. It was appraised and sold at public auction in July 1865, and on August 2 the buildings were declared vacant. Claims by the State Board of Agriculture for damage to the fairgrounds were eventually settled by the federal government for $9,816.56.

Little about the Camp Morton of midsummer 1865 was consistent with residents' memories of old Henderson's Grove or the fairgrounds of 1861. Hundreds of trees had been cut for lumber or firewood, and the earth was pitted and scarred. The city approved some three thousand dollars to go towards the land's rehabilitation.

When it was first sold in 1865, Camp Morton once again became the Indiana State Fairgrounds, but only briefly, until 1890, when a new State Fairgrounds was constructed farther north. The old State Fairgrounds property was then sold off and platted as a residential district. The ditch was supplanted by a part of the city's drainage system, streets were built, and lots were filled with many large and stately houses. This area of Indianapolis is known now as Herron-Morton Place.

In 1916, the first official marking of the old Camp Morton was initiated by students and teachers of Indianapolis School No. 45. They marked the site by placing an inscribed boulder at Alabama and 19th Street.

Four boundary markers were installed on July 15, 2000, by the Sons of Union Veterans of the Civil War, in cooperation with the Sons of Confederate Veterans. A dedication of these markers was conducted in 2003 at a park within the boundaries.

In 1911, Sumner Archibald Cunningham, editor of *Confederate Veteran* magazine, received permission to place a bronze memorial

This is a boundary marker for the southwest corner of Camp Morton, erected in recent years. Geographic boundaries of the prison are all memorialized by these markers. Photo by the author.

tablet in Indianapolis in honor of the popular and humane early Camp Morton commandant, Col. Richard Owen. Contributions flooded in to the extent that a bronze bust of the colonel was substituted for the tablet and was placed in the Indiana State House in Indianapolis. A replica of the bust is located in the Indiana Memorial Union on the campus of Indiana University, Bloomington.

No such monument was ever suggested for Col. Ambrose A.

Stevens, who presided over Camp Morton when it was called "that den of misery a little north of Indianapolis."

W. R. Holloway and Dr. John A. Wyeth had one more public debate, albeit a brief one, in the pages of *Century Monthly Magazine.* Holloway was given an opportunity to answer Dr. Wyeth's "Rejoinder," which had appeared in the magazine, and then Dr. Wyeth got a chance for another short reply. These small articles were essentially restatements of allegations already leveled by both sides.

Following his imprisonment at Camp Morton and his release to return home to Alabama, many years passed before Wyeth was able to fully regain his health. In 1867, though still suffering from the effects of dysentery, typhoid, and malaria, he began studying medicine and opened his practice two years later in his reviving hometown.

But Wyeth soon gave up his practice in despair over the death of a patient and determined to acquire the finest clinical training available during that era. For three years, he worked as a riverboat pilot in Arkansas until he could afford tuition to New York's Bellevue Medical College, where he matriculated in 1872. By the end of the century, Wyeth had become one of the most prominent surgeons in the country, having written a leading surgical textbook, served as president of both the New York Medical Association and the American Medical Association, and established the first postgraduate school of medicine in the country, the Polyclinic Hospital.

Together with his career as surgeon, Wyeth earned a national reputation as a historian and man of letters, publishing several books and numerous articles for *Harper's* and, of course, *Century Monthly.* He is especially known and appreciated in Civil War research circles as the author of the first major biography of Confederate general Nathan Bedford Forrest. This book would stand as the central source for all subsequent biographies of Forrest. Both in his work on Forrest and in the long account of his incarceration at Camp Morton, Wyeth's focus was to document (far more than most historians of his day) the lives of common enlisted soldiers.

Dr. Wyeth, who was selected as a member of the Alabama Hall of Fame for his many contributions to the fields of medicine and literature, died in 1922.

In time, the Camp Morton debate would be forgotten as old wounds from the Civil War began to heal, old Confederate soldiers passed away, and the nation moved on in unity of purpose.

A marker giving a brief history of Camp Morton is located near the entrance to the park now at the prison site. Photo by the author.

A public park now occupies roughly the entrance area to Camp Morton. Today, children play where Confederate soldiers once suffered and died. Photo by the author.

CHAPTER 11

The Legacy of Camp Morton

On a cold, blustery, winter day, I, my then-eleven-year-old son, and my wife walked around a small inner-city park in Indianapolis where the entrance to Camp Morton had once been located. I tried to imagine what it would have been like for a Confederate prisoner of 1864 to stand shivering on a winter day much like this one, wearing only tattered clothing and weakened by illness and malnutrition. But it was difficult to imagine, because the site in Indianapolis that was Camp Morton in 1864 has changed so much since then.

In the latter part of the nineteenth century, the construction of homes began on the spot where thousands of Confederate prisoners had once suffered and many hundreds died. The neighborhood flourished until the Great Depression. But then the economic realities of the 1930s caused many of the homes to be divided into apartments. From the 1950s through the 1970s, many homes were lost to fire and demolition as inner-city decay set in.

But a group of civic leaders and local residents decided that the area was well worth preserving. They established the Herron-Morton Place Neighborhood Association in 1976 to spearhead the renovations of homes, encourage residential development, reduce crime, and rebuild community spirit. In 1983, Herron-Morton Place was listed on the National Register of Historic Places; it became a historical preservation district in 1986.

A part of the restoration of the area is a small park located at roughly the entrance to the old Camp Morton. A modern historic marker telling about the camp is posted there, as well as the large, inscribed granite boulder that was a gift from an Indianapolis school in 1916 to commemorate the site of the prison. Children can swing on swings and families can have picnics at the same spot where young Confederate prisoners once struggled to survive the ravages of starvation and unimaginable physical abuse.

Looking across the park into the surrounding neighborhood on this frigid winter day, I began to reflect upon the circumstances that were responsible for such inhumanity in a so-called "civilized" Northern U.S. city during the 1860s. In my public-school American history courses, I had been taught that the Civil War was about one and only one issue: the terrible and immoral practice of the slavery of African-Americans. But our twenty-first-century perspective makes it difficult to understand the varied and complex reasons why Americans in the nineteenth-century would want to fight and kill one other in battle and torture one another in both Northern and Southern prison camps.

One must travel in time back into the early 1800s to begin to gain a true understanding of what created this animosity that pitted "brother against brother" in a horrific and costly War Between the States. Southerners were growing increasingly unhappy with tariffs that were required to be paid on goods brought into the United States from foreign countries. Southern states imported more goods from overseas than Northern states, so many in the South resented this economic burden.

Taxes were also placed on many Southern goods shipped to foreign countries, an expense that was not always applied to Northern goods of equal value. Southern banks found themselves paying higher interest rates on loans from Northern banks. This situation worsened after several economic "panics," including one in 1857 that affected more Northern banks than Southern. Southern financiers were forced into higher payments to save Northern banks from their own poor investment practices.

Most Americans today would have a hard time understanding the dynamics of geographic sectionalism during the Civil War era. As populations increased in Northern and Midwestern states, the influence of the federal government in Washington, D.C. lessened. Southern states lost political power because the population in the South did not grow as rapidly.

Southern citizens began to believe that state laws carried more weight than federal laws, and their resentment towards the federal government increased. Just as the original thirteen colonies had fought for their freedom from Great Britain nearly a century earlier, Southern states began to talk about rebelling to become free from the federal government's authority in Washington, D.C. This geographic sectionalism became so profound that, during the Civil War, Confederate officers and soldiers often said "my country" when referring to the Southern states.

It is also difficult for many Americans today to understand the South's position on slavery at that time. Why would a section of the nation believe it had a *right* to enslave other human beings?

As terrible as it was, slavery had been a part of life in America since the early colonial period. Southern planters relied on slaves to run plantations and make them profitable, and many slaves were also used to provide labor to run affluent Southern households. Before the Civil War, state and federal laws actually protected the right to purchase and hold slaves.

In their passionate arguments against Northern abolitionists, Southern politicians contended that the U.S. Constitution guaranteed the right to own property and that slaves were "property." Many Southerners believed that slavery should be allowed in new territories such as Kansas and Missouri. This created even greater conflict between Northern abolitionists and Southern politicians.

Emotions had reached a fever pitch when Abraham Lincoln was elected president of the United States in 1860. Lincoln not only vowed to keep the new territories free of slavery, he vowed to keep the nation united under the federal government. On April 12, 1861, the first shots of the war would be fired by Southern cannons on Fort Sumter, South Carolina, and the great and terrible Civil War would begin.

Slavery was undeniably one of the issues that sparked the Civil War, but many historians believe it was not the primary reason that the average Confederate soldier left his home and family to go fight Yankees. Relatively few of the fighting men from the South owned slaves or came from families who did. Slave ownership was primarily limited to wealthy Southern families who produced Confederate generals, not privates and corporals.

The majority of Johnny Rebs went to war under the banner of states' rights. While many did not oppose the institution of slavery, it was not their main motive for fighting. Most viewed the federal government as an oppressive foe and believed that they were participating in the second great revolution in America.

Americans today might also be surprised to learn that many Northern soldiers did not connect their involvement in the war primarily with abolishing slavery—especially in the years prior to

*Some of the soldiers who served as guards at Camp Morton are buried in
this Union veterans' plot in Crown Hill Cemetery. Photo by the author.*

Lincoln's Emancipation Proclamation. In general, they fought for
the main purpose of "preserving the Union." The Union soldiers
who equated their abuse of prisoners at Camp Morton with these
prisoners' treatment of slaves in the South were simply looking for
an excuse to be cruel. Very few true abolitionists populated the
Union Army, especially in regiments formed in the Midwest. Letters
written home during the war frequently included racist statements
from Union soldiers who resented the idea of risking their lives to
free African-Americans from immoral bondage.

But the hostility between soldiers of the North and South was
very real and very intense. Southern soldiers were angry at the
Northern troops because they believed that they were invading
their homeland. Northern soldiers were angry at the Southern
troops because they felt that their rebellion threatened to destroy
the entire nation.

This pervasive anger and resentment certainly found its expression in the treatment of Confederate prisoners at Camp Morton.
The intensity of feeling that spawned such cruelty is difficult to
fathom today, especially in light of the fact that America in the 1860s

was deemed a "Christian nation." But Judeo-Christian morality was certainly found lacking in the harsh treatment and outright abuse of the frail and haggard prisoners at Camp Morton.

What are the lessons to be learned from Camp Morton? One is the danger in governmental and military officials focusing more on self-preservation and self-promotion than on the best interests of the American citizenry. Many influential officials in Indianapolis and Indiana essentially looked the other way while Camp Morton's prisoners were being abused and neglected. They closed the camp to outside scrutiny when conditions became severe. Then, after the war, when men of demonstrated integrity like Dr. Wyeth told of their terrible experiences while imprisoned in the camp, these same officials proclaimed that those ex-prisoners were either not telling the truth or were exaggerating. All of this was done for the primary purpose of protecting reputations of powerful politicians and military leaders.

Another lesson to be learned from Camp Morton is that when American citizens go to war under accepted "just war" principles, we must transcend the impulse to exact revenge and to do cruel deeds to our enemies in anger and hatred. When this occurs, those flying the banner of righteousness lose moral impetus and credibility with other nations of the world.

The story of the men who struggled to stay alive at Camp Morton—and those who died while they were imprisoned there—is important to our nation's history and should never be forgotten.

Yes, Dr. Wyeth, dead men do tell tales.

Appendix

Confederate Prisoners at Camp Morton Who Died There and Who Are Memorialized at Indianapolis's Crown Hill Cemetery

Confederate Burials in Section 32

NAME, MILITARY UNIT, DATE OF DEATH, HOME STATE

ABERCROMBIE, A. E, 2nd Inf. Jan. 22, 1864 SC
ACHREE, P. H. H, 56th Inf. Apr. 7, 1864 VA
ADALAN, A. D. A, Inf. Jul. 4, 1863 LA
ADAMS, A. J. F, 45th Inf. Mar. 5, 1865 AL
ADAMS, Adolphus. E, 8th Bn. Feb. 2, 1865 GA
ADAMS, Frank. B, 3rd Inf. Aug. 18, 1863 KY
ADAMS, J. E., Ward's Bn., Lt. Art. Dec. 2, 1863 AL
ADAMS, John F. C, 52nd Inf. Dec. 11, 1864 GA
ADAMS, S. J. A, 26th Inf. May 24, 1862 MS
ADDIS, John G. D, Williams' Jan. 30, 1865 MO
ADKINS, R. M. G, 51st PR. Feb. 4, 1864 AL
AIKENS, William. C, 9th Cav. Bn. Jul. 27, 1862 TN
AKIN, Anderson J. E, 9th Cav. Bn. TN
ALBERSON, William. B, 5th Inf. GA
ALEXANDER, Benjamin. D, 3rd Inf. Sep. 28, 1863 LA
ALEXANDER, J. F. I, 11th Cav. AL
ALLEN, A. M. I, 39th Inf. Mar. 5, 1864 NC
ALLEN, J. B. K, 10th Inf. Jul. 17, 1864 TX
ALLEN, J. W. D, 10th Cav. Nov. 24, 1863 TN
ALLEN, John. A, Morgan's 2nd Cav. Oct. 31, 1863 KY
ALLEN, John W. G, 56th Inf. Sep. 15, 1863 GA

ALLEN, Lewis. C, 26th Inf. Jul. 7, 1862 TN
ALLEN, R. W. E, 26th Inf. Aug. 22, 1862 TN
ALLFORD, Thomas. B, 56th Inf. Jan. 28, 1865 GA
ALMINDINGER, Henry. B, 1st Hvy. Art. Mar. 18, 1864 LA
AMBURN, John. D, 45th Inf. Jan. 16, 1865 VA
ANDERSON, Allen. D, Colm's Bn. Apr. 26, 1862 TN
ANDERSON, B. J. K, 17th Cav. Mar. 4, 1865 TX
ANDING, W. C. A, 40th Inf. Dec. 14, 1863 MS
ANDREWS, Felix G. H, 33rd Inf. Jul. 15, 1864 MS
ANDREWS, James. I, Fuller's Bat. SC
ARCHER, William. C, 4th Inf. Nov. 27, 1863 MO
ARNHART, G. W. B, Burns' 8th Inf. Jul. 16, 1864 MO
ARNOLD, J. F. D, 25th Inf. May 6, 1865 AL
ARRANTS, S. H. K, 61st Inf. Jul. 30, 1863 TN
ARRINGTON, Samuel. I, 19th Inf. Mar. 19, 1865 AL
ARROWOOD, Andrew J. B, 20th Inf. Feb. 20, 1865 NC
ARSEMENT, Joachim. C, 1st Art. Jan. 16, 1864 LA
ASH, William R. C, 65th Inf. Jan. 11, 1865 GA
ASHWORTH, C. A. K, 53rd Inf. Jul. 3, 1862 TN
ATCHLEY, James F. H, 5th Inf. Nov. 30, 1863 MO
ATNIP, Richard. 1st Bn. Apr. 28, 1862 TN
ATWELL, John. A, 45th Inf. VA
AUCCIN, Theodule. B, 1st Hvy. Art. LA
AVERILL, Jacob. D, 36th Inf. Aug. 23, 1864 VA
AYRES, William. D, 43rd Inf. Mar. 3, 1865 MS
BABB, J. L. B, MD Moreland's Cav. Feb. 9, 1865 AL
BACCUS, C. H. B, 4th Inf. Mar. 29, 1862 MS
BAGWELL, H. B. A, 4th Inf. Feb. 4, 1865 MS
BAIL, Jonathan. F, 36th Inf. VA
BAILEY, Mathias H. H, 60th Inf. Sep. 19, 1864 VA
BAILEY, Nathan. H, Shaler's 27th Inf. Nov. 27, 1864 AR
BAKER, A. J. H, 2nd Inf. Jan. 25, 1864 MO
BAKER, I. N. C, 8th Cav. Jul. 26, 1864 TN
BALDWIN, F. A. B, 60th Inf. Feb. 1, 1865 NC
BALDWIN, J. W. L, 3rd Inf. Nov. 13, 1863 KY
BANKS, John R. B, 33rd Inf. Feb. 15, 1865 MS
BANTA, A. J. H, 1st Butler's Cav. Aug. 20, 1864 KY
BARDING, J. D. H, 5th Cav. Nov. 18, 1863 TN
BARNARD, Samuel E. H, 4th Cav. Mar. 8, 1865 MO
BARNES, E. A, Elliott's Cav. Dec. 15, 1863 MO

BARNES, J. A. K, 8th Inf. Oct 25, 1863 AR

BARNES, J. A, Greer's Bn. TX

BARNETT, Adam H. H, 45th Inf. Mar. 10, 1865 VA

BARNETT, B. F, Cherokee Art. Jan. 20, 1865 GA

BARNETT, Benjamin. C, 2nd Mtd. Inf. Mar. 12, 1862 KY

BARNETT, F. M. D, Greer's Bn. TX

BARNETT, Francis A. F, 45th Inf. Aug. 9, 1864 MS

BARNETT, Henry. C, 26th Inf. MS

BARNETT, James W. E, 3rd Cav. Nov. 28, 1863 AL

BARNETT, Thomas. C, 26th Inf. Apr. 9, 1862 MS

BARNHART, James. E, 1st Cav. MO

BARRY, John. I, 1st Bn. Apr. 25, 1862 AL

BARTLETT, Henry. I, 8th Cav. Jan. 5, 1862 MO

BASDEN, Jesse. C, 5th Cav. Mar. 11, 1865 GA

BASS, Lafayette. J, Cherokee Art. Dec. 4, 1863 GA

BASS, Richard. A, 53rd Inf. Jul. 19, 1862 TN

BASTIAN, Jacob. C, Waul's Legion Jul. 3, 1863 TX

BATES, J. P. G, 4th Inf. May 9, 1862 MS

BATEY, Anderson. G, 42nd Inf. Jul. 10, 1864 AL

BAXTER, Holloway. A, 1st Inf. Nov. 22, 1863 TN

BAZELL, Andrew. D, 17th Inf. Jan. 9, 1864 TX

BEARD, John B. F, 60th Inf. Jul. 9, 1863 TN

BEARD, Perry. I, 26th Inf. Apr. 2, 1862 TN

BEARFIELDS, J. W. Smith's Bat. Apr. 3, 1863 MS

BEASLEY, Samuel. G, 41st Inf. Feb. 15, 1863 AL

BEASTLER, David. C, 28th Inf. Jul. 23, 1863 LA

BEATTIE, James. B, 4th Inf. FL

BEAVERS, M. G, 45th Inf. Jan. 11, 1865 VA

BEDSAUL, George W. C, 47th Cav. Bn. Jan. 25, 1865 VA

BELEW, J. Wesley. F, 3rd Inf. Apr. 4, 1862 MS

BELL, Thomas S. I, 40th Inf. Feb. 17, 1865 GA

BELLAH, H. R. B, 4th Inf. Jul. 18, 1864 GA

BELLAMY, Abner H. A, 52nd Inf. Mar. 10, 1865 VA

BENSON, James. C, 26th Inf. Feb. 11, 1863 TN

BETTERTON, L. M. McClellan's Bat. Nov. 15, 1863 TN

BEVILL, James R. C, Forrest's Cav. Sep. 26, 1864 TN

BIGGS, Thomas. D, 36th Inf. Jan. 28, 1865 MS

BINGHAM, C. D, 36th Inf. Jan. 22, 1865 AL

BINGHAM, Harris. D, 36th Inf. Jan. 27, 1865 AL

BIRD, John. B, Waul's Legion TX

BIRD, William. D, Melton's Cav. Jun. 4, 1862 KY
BISHOP, S. N. B, Russell's 4th Cav. Jul. 16, 1864 AL
BISPHAM, Thomas M. C, 41st Inf. Jun. 19, 1864 AL
BLACK, A. J. C, 26th Inf. Mar. 12, 1862 TN
BLACK, Andrew S. C, Johnston's 1st Inf. Aug. 12, 1862 MS
BLACK, J. O. C, 8th Inf. Bn. Mar. 11, 1865 GA
BLADON, Thomas. A, Inf. Mar. 12, 1862 TN
BLAIN, James C. B, 4th Inf. Mar. 9, 1862 MS
BLAKEMORE, J. Holmes Co., Greer's Cav. TX
BLAKENY, Robert. A, 8th Inf. Feb. 10, 1865 MS
BLANCHARD, Alcee. B, 1st Hvy. Art. Jan. 4, 1864 LA
BLANCHARD, Joseph. B, 1st Hvy. Art. Mar. 19, 1863 LA
BLANKENSHIP, J. A. F, 64th Inf. Aug. 23, 1864 NC
BLANTON, A. H. H, 12th Cav. Jan. 26, 1865 MS
BLANTON, G. M. A, 26th Inf. Apr. 7, 1862 MS
BLESSING, Jacob. A, 12th Inf. Mar. 12, 1865 TN
BLEVIN, Alexander. C, 45th Inf. Sep. 23, 1864 TN
BLEVINS, Henry. K, 26th Inf. Jun. 30, 1862 TN
BLYTHE, William. K, Cooke's Inf. Feb. 22, 1864 AR
BODIE, A. J. C, 7th Inf. Bn. Mar. 2, 1864 MS
BOGEL, James. B, 18th Cav. VA
BOHANAN, Barthello. B, 1st Cav. Oct. 15, 1863 MO
BOHART, W. F, 15th Cav. Oct. 17, 1863 MO
BOONE, B. S. B, 29th Inf. NC
BOONE, Robert E. G, Gordon's Cav. Mar. 14, 1865 MO
BOOSHEE, George W. D, 43rd Inf. NC
BOOTH, George W. H, McGehee's Inf. Mar. 21, 1865 AR
BOOTH, William A. H, 1st Inf. Mar. 4, 1862 GA
BOSWELL, George. C, 63rd Inf. Aug. 24, 1864 GA
BOUDREAUX, Desire. C, 1st Art. Nov. 17, 1863 LA
BOUDREAUX, Maurice. C, 1st Art. Oct. 13, 1863 LA
BOURG, Joachim. C, 1st Art. LA
BOURG, Octave. B, 1st Art. Mar. 5, 1864 LA
BOWEN, James. G, 41st Inf. Aug. 12, 1864 TN
BOWLING, John R. K, 26th Inf. Mar. 18, 1862 TN
BOWMAN, Elias. I, 45th Inf. Feb. 21, 1865 VA
BOWMAN, N. C. K, 18th Inf. Mar. 19, 1865 AL
BOYD, Joseph A. B, 3rd Cav. Dec. 26, 1863 MO
BOYD, Z. I. H, 4th Inf. Mar. 7, 1862 MS
BRABHAM, William. B, 33rd Inf. Jan. 25, 1865 MS

BRADFORD, Samuel. H, 43rd Inf. Jul. 19, 1863 TN
BRADFORD, William. I, 41st Inf. Sep. 12, 1862 TN
BRADLEY, Josiah M. K, 32nd Inf. Mar. 16, 1863 AL
BRADLEY, William G. K, 32nd Inf. Mar. 22, 1863 AL
BRADSHAW, John H. F, Thomas's Legion Dec. 16, 1864 NC
BRAFFORD, A. H. B, 53rd Inf. Sep. 6, 1864 TN
BRALTON, Albert. C, Melton's Cav. Mar. 10, 1862 KY
BRAMLETTE, Josiah. C, 1st Inf. TX
BRAND, John J. K, 15th Cav. Jan. 14, 1865 AL
BRANSCOMB, F. C. C. E, 45th Inf. Feb. 22, 1865 VA
BRANTLEY, E. R. G, 15th Inf. Feb. 9, 1865 AL
BRATTON, A. M, Melton's Cav. Mar. 27, 1862 KY
BRAZILLE, Samuel A. A, 50th Inf. Jan. 17, 1864 TN
BREWER, C. C. H, Nixon's 48th Inf. Mar. 11, 1865 TN
BRICE, John B. H, 1st Cav. AR
BRICE, W. W. Corput's Co., Lt. Art. GA
BRICKER, J. C, 51st Inf. Feb. 22, 1863 TN
BRILES, H. B, 9th Inf. Nov. 10, 1863 AR
BRINGLE, Christian. H, 32nd Inf. Apr. 3, 1864 TN
BRITT, Alfred. C, 7th Inf. Bn. Aug. 20, 1863 MS
BROCKER, S. L. F, 1st Butler's Cav. KY
BRON, Thomas. G, 1st Inf. Jan. 26, 1865 GA
BROOKS, J. W. D, 61st Inf. Jul. 5, 1863 TN
BROOKS, John T. A, 1st Cav. Feb. 7, 1864 LA
BROOMS, J. S. B, 37th Inf. Jan. 5, 1865 MS
BROTHERTON, Thomas. I, 1st Inf. Nov. 6, 1864 GA
BROUGHMAN, H. J. F, 60th Inf. Oct. 4, 1864 VA
BROUSSARD, Meonce. I, 1st Art. Dec. 23, 1863 LA
BROWN, Andrew J. A, 2nd Inf. Feb. 20, 1864 MO
BROWN, Aug. Y. E, 36th Inf. Jul. 2, 1864 MS
BROWN, J. A. H, McGehee's Inf. Jan. 30, 1865 AR
BROWN, John E. K, 16th Inf. Apr. 20, 1863 LA
BROWN, M. A. B, 26th Inf. Apr. 10, 1862 TN
BROWN, N. A, 24th Inf. Feb. 13, 1865 SC
BROWN, N. L. B, 53rd Inf. Mar. 24, 1862 TN
BROWN, Richard. K, Anderson's Inf. Bn. NC
BROWN, Samuel. F, 15th Inf. Jan. 2, 1864 AR
BROWN, W. G. B, 60th Inf. Oct. 20, 1863 NC
BROWN, W. S. B, 59th Inf. Dec. 20, 1864 TN
BROWN, William F. C, 25th Inf. Jan. 22, 1865 GA

BROWNING, A. J. D, 45th Bn. Oct. 30, 1864 VA
BRUNER, John M. K, 1st Inf. Aug. 8, 1862 MS
BRYANT, A. O. K, 4th Inf. Mar. 26, 1862 MS
BYSON, William Y. E, 52nd Inf. Jul. 3, 1864 GA
BUCHANAN, James H. D, 45th Inf. Nov. 6, 1864 VA
BUCK, T. J. K, Harris's Cav. LA
BUCKNER, W. O. G, McIntosh's Indian
BUFORD, A. M. B, 63rd Inf. Oct. 25, 1864 GA
BUFORD, James Thomas. C, 2nd Mtd. Inf. Mar. 22, 1862 KY
BUGG, Robert H. B, 56th Inf. Mar. 8, 1862 VA
BULLARD, H. K, Coffee's Inf. MO
BULLOCK, D. D. B, 1st Inf. Dec. 22, 1863 LA
BULWARK, H. F, 2nd Inf. Jun. 18, 1863 TN
BURDEN, G. W. B, 29th Cav. TX
BURGAN, Nathaniel. Harris's Inf. Bn. MO
BURGESS, Edward. A, 8th Cav. Jun. 23, 1864 TN
BURGOYNE, Thomas H. D, 26th Inf. Oct. 19, 1864 AR
BURKE, Patrick. G, William's Bat. Mar. 1, 1864 TN
BURKS, J. H. G, 12th Inf. Nov. 17, 1863 AL
BURNETT, J. J, Forrest's Cav. May 20, 1862 TN
BURNETT, W. O. E, 5th Inf. Jul. 13, 1864 TN
BURNS, Alonzo W. G, 16th Cav. Oct 25, 1863 GA
BURNS, C. A. Mar. 19, 1864
BURNS, J. J. H, 9th Art. Jun. 13, 1863 KY
BURTON, Christopher. G, 28th Inf. Jun. 23, 1863 TN
BURTON, Daniel W. Wisdom's Co., Forrest's Cav. TN
BUTCHER, James. Love's Cav. Feb. 16, 1864 LA
BUTLER, H. J, Newsom's Cav. Nov. 29, 1863 AL
BUTLER, William. H, 3rd Inf. Mar. 14, 1864 MO
BYRD, George B. C, 12th Inf. May 5, 1864 LA
CABOS, John B. H, 1st Bat. LA
CAGLE, David. H, 49th Inf. Jun. 9, 1864 AL
CAISON, J. H. K, 15th Inf. Jan. 9,1864 AL
CALDWELL, Lawson. A, 62nd Inf. Jan. 30, 1864 NC
CALLOWAY, Charles A. E, 1st Cav. MO
CAMERON, James. C, 4th Inf. Mar. 2, 1862 TN
CAMPBELL, A. K. G, 4th Inf. Oct. 16,1863 MS
CAMPBELL, Alfred. F, 27th Inf. Nov. 23, 1863 AL
CAMPBELL, J. D, 33rd Inf. Feb. 17, 1865 TN
CAMPBELL, J. R. Forrest's Cav. Mar. 22, 1864 TN

CAMPBELL, J. R. K, 4th Inf. Jan. 2, 1864 TN
CAMPBELL, James D. F, 1st Cav. Jan. 2, 1864 TN
CAMPBELL, William. C, 33rd Inf. Feb. 19, 1865 TN
CANNON, John M. B, 8th Bn. Jan. 11, 1865 GA
CANNON, L. A, 13th Cav. Bn. Feb. 16, 1865 LA
CANTENBURY, D. C. C, William's Bn. Feb. 24, 1865 AL
CANTRILL, John T. H, 2nd Inf. Apr. 1, 1862 KY
CANTWELL, William. G, 5th Cav. Aug. 23, 1864 TN
CAPEHART, P. M. A, 4th Bn. Feb. 1, 1864 LA
CARLISLE, R. C. H, 9th Cav. Mar. 6, 1865 AL
CARNELL, J. N. I, 2nd Inf. AR
CARPENTER, Moses. C, Roddey's Cav. Jul. 26, 1864 AL
CARR, John. C, 4th Inf. Feb. 20, 1864 TN
CARROLL, A. B. A, 7th Inf. Nov. 21, 1863 KY
CARROLL, Dennis. C, 4th Cav. Jan. 25, 1864 GA
CARROLL, Rufus. H, 27th Bn. Feb. 10, 1865 VA
CARROLL, William B. F, 3rd Inf. MS
CARRY, J. A. F, 4th Cav. Feb. 13,1865 GA
CARTER, William. H, 3rd Inf. Mar. 2, 1862 MS
CARTWRIGHT, William D. K, 45th Inf. Feb. 20, 1865 VA
CARTY, W. L. G, 34th Inf. Jan. 26, 1864 AL
CASEY, Baxter. G, 64th Inf. NC
CASHION, Samuel C. C, 53rd Inf. Feb. 27, 1862 TN
CASHON, P. D. C, 4th Cav. Dec. 6, 1863 GA
CASSIDY, Samuel. D, 27th Inf. Dec. 21, 1864 AL
CASTEEL, M. V. H, 3rd Inf. Aug. 12, 1864 MO
CASTELLO, Thomas. D, 20th Inf. Aug. 7, 1864 LA
CATANNE, Molo. B, 1st Zouaves LA
CATES, R. L, Barry's Bat. TN
CAULEY, Simeon. I, 40th Inf. Dec. 15, 1864 GA
CAVENER, Thomas J. E, 53rd Inf. Aug. 4, 1863 TN
CENTENO, Alce. C, 23rd Inf. Jul. 8, 1864 LA
CENTER, J. S. W. I, 26th Inf. Aug. 30, 1862 TN
CENTERS, Morgan. A, 19th Inf. Jun. 8, 1865 TN
CERTAIN, Thomas L. A, 1st Bat. Jul. 25, 1862 TN
CHADWICK, H. H. H, 5th Bn. Oct. 14, 1863 MO
CHANCEY, Joseph. A, Lewis's Cav. Bn.
CHAPMAN, Thrashley. H, 37th Inf. Dec. 30, 1864 MS
CHAPMAN, W. T. C, 8th Inf. Apr. 28, 1862 KY
CHAPMAN, William. C, 11th Inf. Dec. 4, 1863 MO

CHATHAM, Noah C. E, 3rd Inf. Jan. 11, 1864 MS
CHATMAN, Isaac F. E, 41st Inf. Dec. 16, 1864 GA
CHEETY, J. N. W. E, 56th Inf. Mar. 31, 1862 VA
CHELLETT, Christy. D, 12th Inf. LA
CHERRY, Wilson H. B, Cav. Aug. 16, 1863 KY
CHESTNUT, Alexander. B, 4th Inf. Mar. 4, 1862 MS
CHEWNING, Richard. B, 2nd Inf. Dec. 4, 1864 MS
CHILDRESS, G. E. A, Eng. Corps. AL
CHRISTIAN, J. H. E, 45th Inf. Mar. 26, 1865 VA
CHRONISTER, Isham. E, 15th NW Inf. Feb. 18, 1864 AR
CLARK, A. C, Melton's Cav. Aug. 20, 1862 KY
CLARK, G. W. C, 59th Inf. Jan. 13, 1865 TN
CLARK, John C, 1st Cav. Aug. 20, 1864 TN
CLARK, Washington. B, Hamilton's Cav. Mar. 18, 1864 TN
CLARK, William. A, 2nd Inf. TX
CLARK, William M. C. A, 41st Inf. Feb. 6, 1863 AL
CLARKSON, Henry. C, 60th Inf. Dec. 8, 1864 VA
CLAUNCH, G. B. H, 26th Inf. Apr. 4, 1862 MS
CLAY, J. W. D, 37th Cav. Bn. Jul. 7, 1864 VA
CLAYBORN, C. Mar. 5, 1863
CLAYLAND, E. W, 2nd Inf. Mar. 9, 1863 KY
CLAYTON, James P. A, 43rd Inf. Aug. 12, 1864 GA
CLAYTON, Sampson. C, Johnston's 1st Inf. MS
CLEASE, D. L. C, 1st Cav. Jan. 4, 1865 TN
CLEVER, M. G, 8th Cav. Mar. 2, 1864 AR
CLONE, Almew. 6th Inf. Aug. 15, 1862 KY
CLONE, J. Melton's Cav. May 24, 1862 KY
CLORK, W. M. G, 1st Inf. TN
COAKER, Russell. C, 44th Inf. Dec. 23, 1863 AL
COAST, John. B, 13th Inf. LA
COBBS, W. M. Dec. 5, 1863 KY
COBURN, A. I, Butler's 1st Cav. May 15, 1864 KY
COCHRAN, William. G, 26th Inf. MS
COCHRAN, William R. G, 26th Inf. Apr. 2, 1862 MS
COFER, James A. D, 1st Cav. Mar. 24,1864 MO
COFIELD, S. B. H, 7th Cav. Dec. 6, 1863 AL
COGGINS, A. F, 61st Inf. Jun. 21, 1863 TN
COINER, Charles. E, 1st Inf. VA
COLEMAN, Robert. A, Patton's 21st Inf. LA
COLEMAN, T. J. D, Allison's Legion TN

COLEMAN, T. J. I, 2nd Cav. Jul. 31, 1864 KY
COLEMAN, W. A. B, 41st Inf. Mar. 24, 1862 TN
COLLINS, Jacob. I, 3rd Inf. Apr. 20, 1865 MS
COLLINS, John T. K, 2nd Inf. Jul. 21, 1862 KY
COLLINS, W. H. H, 41st Inf. Mar. 3, 1862 TN
CONNOR, Despalier. I, 1st Horse Art. Nov. 20, 1863 LA
CONROY, John. C, Johnston's 10th Cav. Jan. 26, 1865 KY
COOK, Eli. G, 10th Cav. Jan. 22, 1865 KY
COOK, Francis M. G, 26th Inf. Aug. 17, 1862 MS
COOK, J. W. A, 46th Inf. Feb. 5, 1865 MS
COOK, James H. D, 31st Inf. Oct. 21, 1864 MS
COOK, Marcus. I, 1st Cav. TN
COOK, N. B. A, 8th Mo. Jul. 14, 1864 MO
COOK, R. F. G, 25th Inf. Feb. 18, 1863 LA
COOK, William A. A, 19th Inf. Jan. 24, 1865 TN
COOK, William L. G, 26th Inf. Jul. 8, 1864 MS
COOLEY, Nelson. C, 7th Inf. Bn. Dec. 31, 1864 MS
COON, W. S. B, 41st Inf. Feb. 28, 1865 MS
COOPER, John E. F, 4th Cav. Nov. 15, 1863 GA
COOPER, R. C. D, 1st SS Nov. 1, 1863 GA
COOPER, Russell. D, 29th Inf. Jan. 22, 1865 GA
COOPER, William. A, 16th Cav. Bn. Nov. 8, 1863 GA
COPELAND, P. D. G, Olmstead's 1st Inf. Jul. 30, 1864 GA
CORDELL, L. B. H, 29th Inf. Jul. 21, 1864 NC
CORNETT, Watson. F, 5th Mtd. Inf. Sep. 20, 1864 KY
COUSINS, John R. K, 37th Inf. Mar. 19, 1865 MS
COVERT, L. R. I, 2nd Inf. AR
COVINGTON, W. F. D, 24th Inf. Jan. 24, 1865 TN
COWART, J. T. H, Armistead's Cav. Jul. 26, 1864 MS
COWLES, Jesse. I, 10th Inf. KY
COX, G. C, 45th Inf. VA
COX, William. C, 1st Cav. TN
COX, William. H, Graves' Bat. KY
COZZART, Charles. F, 4th Inf. Mar. 22, 1862 MS
CRABTREE, John W. B, 45th Inf. Bn. Aug. 13, 1864 VA
CRAIG, E. E. H, 10th Cav. Jan. 24, 1864 AR
CRAIG, T. C. H, 8th Inf. Feb. 23, 1864 AR
CRANE, J. P. 1st Confederate Cav.
CRANLEY, Moses. A, 56th Inf. Feb. 21, 1865 TN
CRAWFORD, J. J. Algiers Co., Napier Cav. Feb. 21, 1865 TN

CRAWFORD, John. E, 26th Inf. TN
CRAWFORD, Uriah F. F, 60th Inf. Jan. 16, 1865 VA
CREMIN, J. A, 47th Inf. Jul. 23, 1864 GA
CRENSHAW, William W. A, 31st Inf. May 27, 1864 MS
CRETSINGER, Jacob R. G, 29th Inf. TN
CREWS, Moses. D, 24th Inf. TN
CRIGHFIELD, John. M, Richardson's Cav. TN
CROSBY, G. J. B, 1st Art. TN
CROSS, J. M. E, 3rd Inf. Feb. 22, 1864 TN
CROW, John. B, 15th Inf. Feb. 10, 1864 AR
CROW, Joseph F. C, 31st Inf. Nov. 23, 1863 AL
CRUSE, J. C. B, 9th Inf. Mar. 1, 1864 AR
CRUSSELL, Thomas M. F, 59th Inf. Sep. 18, 1863 TN
CULLINS, A. W. D, 1st Inf. Mar. 16, 1862 TN
CUNNINGHAM, George. E, 48th Inf. AL
CUNNINGHAM, Matthew. H, Walker's Inf. Bn. Feb. 11, 1865 NC
CUNNINGHAM, W. I, 2nd Inf. TX
CUNNINGHAM, W. H. K, 3rd Inf. Jul. 11, 1863 TN
CURLEY, John H. E, 15th Inf. Jan. 30, 1864 TN
CURTIS, B. F. E, 4th Inf. Mar. 9, 1862 MS
DALTON, Amos. H, Hampton's Legion Mar. 23, 1864 SC
DALTON, C. G. I, 45th Inf. Aug. 8, 1864 VA
DANIEL, William B. G, 16th Cav. Bn. Nov. 17, 1863 GA
DANIELS, E. L. H, 8th Inf. Mar. 31, 1862 KY
DANIELS, James D. F, 1st Inf. FL
DANIELS, Robert. 4th Inf. Aug. 7, 1862 MS
DANLEY, John. H, 3rd Cav. Apr. 11, 1865 AR
DARBY, R. R. D, 3rd Inf. FL
DAVID, W. J. F, Shaler's Inf. Feb. 20, 1864 AR
DAVIS, Amos. 1st Inf. Aug. 19, 1863 TN
DAVIS, C. L, 1st Inf. TN
DAVIS, E. C. G, 63rd Inf. Jan. 5, 1864 VA
DAVIS, E. G. G, 36th Inf. Feb. 13, 1865 MS
DAVIS, Ellis. F, 45th Inf. Apr. 11, 1863 AL
DAVIS, Franklin M. H, 20th Cav. TX
DAVIS, George. I, 37th Inf. Dec. 14, 1863 AL
DAVIS, James. E, 35th Inf. Feb. 1, 1865 MS
DAVIS, R. W. C, 31st Inf. Mar. 12, 1862 MS
DAVIS, Robert N. I, 4th Inf. Nov. 28, 1863 MS
DAVIS, Thomas. C, 2nd Inf. Dec. 13, 1863 MO

DAVIS, W. S. A, 1st Cav. Jan. 5, 1864 LA
DAVIS, William P. D, 3rd Inf. Mar. 22, 1864 LA
DAWSON, Muse. E, 52nd Inf. TN
DEAN, Alexander. E, 56th Inf. Mar. 16, 1862 VA
DEAN, B. P. K, 15th Inf. MO
DEAN, E. P, 4th Inf. Bn. Sep. 19, 1863 LA
DEAN, Joseph. B, Cooper's Cav. TN
DEATHRAGE, N. A, 26th Inf. Jul. 15, 1862 TN
DEAVER, John. 29th Inf. NC
DE GROTE, John. Helms' 1st Cav. Aug. 20, 1862 KY
DELAUGHTER, Absalom. D, Grinstead's 33rd Inf. AR
DEMOYS, James. 1st Inf. Bn. Jan. 16, 1864 LA
DENHAM, D. D. D, 52nd Inf. Feb. 19, 1864 TN
DENNING, James. C, 42nd Inf. Dec. 1, 1864 TN
DENNIS, J. W. D, 46th Inf. Jun. 12, 1864 AL
DENNISON, A. Jackson. I, 20th Cav. Jan. 25, 1865 VA
DENTON, James P. E, 12th Cav. Mar. 16, 1865 KY
DESHAYES, Louis. Anderson's Lt. Art. Jun. 15, 1862 GA
DETTER, William. D, 35th Inf. Jan. 29, 1865 MS
DEWBERRY, Henry. F, 25th Inf. AL
DEWEES, Hiram. A, 4th Cav. Jan. 25, 1864 AL
DEYERLES, Charles. D, 5th Inf. Feb. 4, 1865 VA
DICKERSON, J. H. K, 61st Inf. Jun. 16, 1863 TN
DICKERSON, James H. B, 12th Cav. Aug. 14, 1864 TN
DICKERSON, William W. B, 10th Inf. Feb. 14, 1864 TN
DICKEY, James H. D, 32nd Inf. TN
DICKINSON, William J. G, 23rd Inf. Jun. 25, 1864 AR
DICKSON, Robert. H, 32nd Inf. Mar. 7, 1863 AL
DICKSON, Thomas J. D, Hampton's Legion SC
DILLARD, R. M. G, 9th Cav. Jan. 31, 1864 TN
DILLSHA, Levi. E, 53rd Inf. TN
DINWIDDIE, John C. B, Fristoe's Cav. Jan. 18, 1865 MO
DISMUKE, John. B, 4th Inf. Jun. 3, 1862 MS
DOGGETT, John R. D, 53rd Inf. Mar. 29, 1862 TN
DOGGETT, William H. H, 59th Inf. Sep. 2, 1864 TN
DOLL, David F. VA
DORER, W. G, 5th Inf. Jan. 26, 1865 SC
DORSEY, J. K. B, 20th Inf. Dec. 2, 1863 TX
DOSS, H. R. H, 4th Inf. Apr. 6, 1862 MS
DOTSON, Presley P. H, 32nd Inf. Apr. 6, 1862 TN

DOUGLAS, George F. E, 9th Inf. Sep. 16, 1864 TN
DOUGLASS, J. H, Russell's 4th Cav. Jan. 20, 1864 AL
DOWNIE, Thomas. H, 1st Inf. Sep. 5, 1863 MS
DRIGGERS, John. A, 53rd Inf. Jun. 21, 1863 AL
DRURY, John. K, 36th Inf. Jan. 30, 1865 VA
DUBRALL, L. N. E, 40th Inf. Mar. 19, 1864 AL
DUFFIE, George M. I, 22nd Inf. Feb. 17, 1863 AL
DUFFY, John. I, 1st Hvy. Art. Sep. 2, 1863 LA
DUGGINS, Kendrick. A, 4th Cav. KY
DUKE, George. W, Cherokee Art. Jun. 2, 1864 GA
DUKE, William. H, 20th Inf. Mar. 21, 1865 MS
DUNBAR, George. 63rd Inf. Dec. 27, 1864 VA
DUNBAR, William. A, 32nd Inf. Aug. 29, 1864 LA
DUNCAN, G. W. B, 26th Inf. Mar. 18, 1862 MS
DUNCAN, W. M. A, 1st Bn. Mtd. Rifles Mar. 26, 1865 KY
DUPREE, Ferdinand. B, 1st Hvy. Art. Feb. 5, 1864 LA
DURCUSSE, Henry. E, 30th Inf. Feb. 19, 1864 LA
DUTY, James. B, 45th Inf. Jan. 5, 1865 VA
EAKES, Daniel M. K, 54th Inf. VA
EARLEY, J. S. A, 20th Inf. Jun. 13, 1863 MS
EARLY, V. G, 37th Inf. Feb. 13, 1865 MS
EARP, L. W. D, 39th Inf. Jul. 20, 1864 GA
EASTWOOD, Ivy S. C, 8th Inf. KY
EASTWOOD, Samuel L. C, 4th Inf. MS
EATON, J. W. E, 10th Inf. Feb. 28, 1865 TX
EDGE, Edward. A, 50th Inf. Feb. 26, 1864 TN
EDWARDS, Charles B. D, 8th Inf. Mar. 31, 1862 KY
EDWARDS, E. A. C, 8th Inf. KY
EDWARDS, R. R. B, 36th Inf. Mar. 3, 1865 TN
EDWARDS, Robert C. I, Johnston's 1st Inf. Feb. 28, 1862 MS
EDWARDS, W. D. I, 26th Inf. Mar. 21, 1862 MS
EHLERS, Henry. I, Olmstead's 1st Inf. Aug. 27, 1864 GA
EIDSON, J. H. C, 63rd Inf. Dec. 30, 1864 GA
EILAND, J. C. F, 33rd Inf. GA
EISON, Hair. A, 3rd Inf. Jul. 14, 1863 KY
ELAM, Peter C. H, 4th Inf. Mar. 8, 1862 MS
ELI, William. Ratliff's Guerrillas Jul. 27, 1862 KY
ELKINS, Hiram E. I, Crip's Inf. Feb. 24, 1865 AR
ELLIS, Martin A. I, 44th Inf. Jan. 17, 1864 AL
ELLIS, W. B. B, 26th Inf. MS

ELLISON, H. C, 1st Inf. Jul. 28, 1863 TN
ELLISON, R. C. G, 26th Inf. Mar. 9, 1862 TN
ELMORE, Daniel. A, 1st Inf. Bn. May 13, 1862 TN
ELY, Frank K. A, 27th Cav. Bn. Aug. 2, 1864 VA
EMERSON, Joseph H. D, 53rd Inf. Mar. 26, 1862 TN
EMMONS, I. C. G, 34th Inf. Feb. 9, 1865 GA
EMORY, J. P. I, 4th Inf. Mar. 26, 1862 MS
ENGLISH, Willis M. A, 32nd Inf. TN
ENOCH, Sidney. A, 25th Cav. Jan. 11, 1865 VA
EPPERSON, A. P. C, 42nd Cav. Bn. VA
ERVIN, G. W. G, Thomas's 28th Inf. Feb. 3, 1864 LA
ERVIN, George W. E, 1st Mtd. Rifles KY
ESPIROSA, Manuel. D, 30th Inf. Mar. 11, 1864 LA
ETTER, Andrew. D, 5th Cav. Jun. 15, 1864 TN
EUBANKS, Jesse M. D, 2nd Bn. SS Feb. 11, 1865 GA
EVANS, B. S. G, 16th Cav. Jul. 23, 1864 GA
EVANS, Jesse C. H, 4th Inf. Apr. 26, 1865 MS
EVANS, S. W. D, 12th Cav. May 16, 1865 KY
EVANS, T. W. F, 4th Inf. Feb. 25 1862 MS
EVANS, Thomas N. F, 6th Inf. Feb. 4, 1865 VA
EVANS, William A. A, 2nd Inf. Sep. 15, 1863 MO
EVERETT, Thomas P. I, 3rd Inf. Aug. 11, 1864 MS
EVINS, Jasper. I, 48th Inf. Apr. 26, 1865 AL
FAIRCHILD, W. A. A, 5th Cav. Feb. 4 ,1864 TN
FANNING, Jefferson. E, 1st Cav. Oct. 18, 1862 MO
FANNON, O. C. F, 45th Inf. Aug. 8, 1864 VA
FARLACE, James. C, 4th Inf. Dec. 19, 1863 TN
FARLOW, W. A. D, Hawkins' Cav. TN
FARMER, B. F. K, 3rd Inf. Jan. 26, 1864 MS
FARMER, D. A. D, Olmstead's 1st Inf. Feb. 25, 1865 GA
FARMER, E. O. A, 10th Cav. TX
FARMER, John L. I, 10th Cav. Aug. 17, 1864 MO
FARREL, James S. I, 2nd Inf. KY
FARRIS, James. D, 26th Inf. Mar. 24, 1862 MS
FARRISH, J. M. Cav. TX
FAUGHTNER, John. E, 1st Cav. VA
FAULKNER, Thomas. H, 17th Inf. Feb. 8, 1865 VA
FEAGAN, D. W. F, 23rd Inf. MS
FELTO, John. C, 20th Inf. Feb. 14, 1863 TN
FELTS, A. B. A, 26th Inf. Mar. 21, 1862 MS

FERGUS, C. B. B, 2nd Inf. Nov. 15, 1864 MS
FERGUSON, David. A, 36th Inf. KY
FERGUSON, Pat H. G, 63rd Inf. Jan. 22, 1865 GA
FERRELL, C. E. E, 24th Inf. Sep. 22, 1863 SC
FERRELL, Jesse. B, 1st Inf. Feb. 20, 1865 GA
FIFE, W. T. H, 31st Inf. Jul. 29, 1863 MS
FIGHTMASTER, F. M. E, 5th Cav. Feb. 14, 1865 KY
FIGUNE, Manuel. E, 16th Inf. Aug. 15, 1863 LA
FILBY, J. N. K, 2nd Inf. Oct. 9, 1863 TX
FINCHER, William A. E, 17th Inf. Jan. 24, 1865 AL
FINDLEY, F. J. E, 3rd Cav. Dec. 16, 1864 KY
FINK, Stephen. F, 54th Inf. Jan. 12, 1865 VA
FINLEY, Jeremiah. G, 36th Inf. Mar. 19, 1865 VA
FISHER, H. A. J. H, 36th Inf. Dec. 12, 1864 VA
FITZGERALD, G. M. C, 1st Art. Jan. 26, 1864 TN
FITZHUGH, James. I, Hawthorne's Inf. Sep. 23, 1864 AR
FLACK, W. M. F, 1st Inf. Mar. 18, 1862 MS
FLAHERTY, Michael. Cleburne's Inf. AR
FLAMMEX, John. B, 31st Inf. TN
FLANIGAN, Seaburn W. E, 20th Inf. GA
FLETCHER, William. A, 1st Cav. Jan. 25, 1864 LA
FLIPPO, Joseph M. D, 32nd Inf. Apr. 9, 1862 TN
FLOYD, F. J. H, 6th Inf. Jan. 25, 1864 MS
FOHNER, D. C, Waul's Legion TX
FONDER, W. H. B, 35th Inf. Jan. 10, 1865 TN
FONDER, W. H. B, 35th Inf. Jan. 16, 1865 TN
FONTENOT, Justin. F, 30th Inf. LA
FORD, Z. K, Russell's 4th Cav. AL
FOREHAND, Amos M. E, 51st Inf. Dec. 2, 1864 GA
FORESTER, John. I, 16th Inf. Mar. 19, 1865 SC
FOSTER, G.W. B, 1st Inf. Jan. 29, 1865 GA
FOSTER, J. F, Holman's Cav. Bn. Dec. 6, 1863 TN
FOSTER, Jonathan. F, 4th Inf. Bn. Jan. 29, 1865 LA
FOSTER, Joseph W. D, 18th Inf. VA
FOUVELL, S. A. C, 17th Inf. Oct. 31, 1864 TN
FOWLER, Augustus. H, 41st Inf. Oct. 10, 1864 TN
FOWLER, James T. F, 26th Inf. Mar. 15, 1862 TN
FRANKLIN, James H. B, 8th Inf. Bn. Jan. 29, 1865 NC
FRANKLIN, W. H. D, Greer's Inf. Bn. TX
FRAZIER, William. B, 2nd Inf. Mar. 12, 1862 KY

FREEMAN, Joel. W, 1st Stireman's Cav. Bn. Nov. 6, 1863 AR
FREEMAN, L. A, 29th Inf. Apr. 17, 1863 NC
FRENCH, W. J. K, 4th Inf. Jan. 11, 1865 TN
FRIEND, Andrew. H, 27th Inf. Dec. 23, 1863 AR
FRIEND, M. T. F, 60th Inf. Feb. 13, 1865 VA
FRISBY, John R. H, 6th Inf. Oct. 13, 1863 MO
FULFORD, William. D, 45th Inf. Dec. 19, 1864 VA
GAINES, Julius. H, 2nd Cav. Sep. 14, 1864 KY
GALE, J. L. B. H, Elliott's Inf. Bn. Jan. 10, 1865 MO
GALE, Robert. H, Elliott's Inf. Bn. Jan. 4, 1865 MO
GAMMONS, Charles H. G, 2nd Mtd. Rifles Jun 30,1864 AR
GAMMONS, R. A. A, 1st Cav. Jun. 30, 1864 LA
GANNAWAY, S. S. D, 51st Inf. Feb. 10, 1864 LA
GARDNER, John. I, 15th Inf. Jul. 22, 1864 TN
GARDNER, Joseph. F, 2nd Choctaw
GARRETT, William. I, 29th Inf. Mar. 24, 1865 AL
GASSET, James. F, 59th Inf. Aug. 11, 1864 TN
GASTON, G. W. H, 10th Cav. Aug. 7, 1864 MO
GATELY, J. W. D, 15th NW Inf. Aug. 29,1863 AR
GATLIN, John. B, 1st Art. Feb. 20, 1864 TN
GAUDY, William R. C, 4th Inf. FL
GAUN, Thomas G. F, 32nd Inf. Jan. 7, 1865 MS
GEARHART, Alexander. D, 10th Inf. Aug. 10, 1864 KY
GEARY, Patrick. F, 30th Inf. Jun. 25, 1864 GA
GENTRY, A. J. G, 4th Inf. Feb. 27, 1862 MS
GEORGE, W. A. D, 41st Inf. Jan. 2, 1865 TN
GIBSON, William G. A, 43rd Inf. Aug. 19, 1864 AL
GILL, J. H. D, 9th Cav. Bn. Jan. 6, 1865 TN
GILL, M. T. K, 39th Inf. Sep. 15, 1863 GA
GILL, William E. D, 9th Inf. Jul. 15, 1862 TN
GILLAM, Ison. E, 10th Inf. Jul. 31, 1864 KY
GILLUM, Richard. Field's Co. Jul. 23, 1864 KY
GILMER, William E. I, 2nd Inf. May 30, 1865 MO
GILMORE, L. M. H, 26th Inf. Apr. 19, 1862 MS
GILMORE, William T. D, 9th Inf. Bn. TN
GLASGOW, C. M. A, 50th Inf. Apr. 6, 1864 TN
GOODSON, Elijah. D, 45th Inf. Feb. 9, 1865 VA
GOODSON, Uzriel. E, 6th Inf. Dec. 28, 1863 SC
GORDON, J. M. F, 48th Inf. Feb. 11, 1865 NC
GORDY, A. E, 6th Inf. Jan. 8, 1865 MS

GORDY, O. E, 6th Inf. Dec. 3, 1864 MS
GOSNEY, Charles. C, 1st Butler's Cav. May 7, 1864 KY
GRACE, David H. K, 3rd Inf. Jul. 8, 1864 MS
GRAHAM, A. E, 1st Inf. Aug. 8, 1862 TN
GRAHAM, George W. K, 54th Inf. Mar. 11, 1865 VA
GRANDIN, J. B. B, 1st Art. Nov. 25, 1863 LA
GRAVELY, Isaac. I, 45th Inf. Aug. 5, 1864 VA
GRAVES, F. A. D, 24th Inf. Jul. 31, 1864 AR
GRAY, Andrew G. F, 36th Inf. Aug. 10, 1864 VA
GRAY, Benjamin. E, 63rd Inf. Sep. 5, 1864 GA
GRAY, Enos. D, 62nd Inf. Oct. 16, 1863 NC
GRAY, J. M. A, 3rd Cav. GA
GRAY, J. W. K, 11th Inf. Nov. 22, 1864 GA
GRAY, James M. E, 7th Cav. Feb. 14, 1865 TN
GREEN, A. B. B, 3rd Cav. Dec. 20, 1863 AL
GREEN, Isaac S. L, 58th Inf. Feb. 13, 1865 NC
GREEN, John E. H, 25th Inf. Dec. 19, 1863 AR
GREEN, O. G. B, 26th Inf. Mar. 21, 1862 MS
GREEN, R. S. C, Cooper's Inf. Jan. 18, 1864 TN
GREEN, William R. H, 25th Inf. Feb. 9, 1864 AR
GREGG, J. P. I, 60th Inf. Jun. 23, 1863 TN
GREGORY, H. C. D, 21st Cav. Jan. 1, 1864 TX
GREGORY, John. H, 66th Inf. Jan. 22, 1865 GA
GRIFFIN, Ebenezer. H, 4th Inf. Oct. 13, 1863 GA
GRIFFIN, Ira W. I, 4th Inf. Jul. 6, 1862 MS
GRIFFITH, H. P. F, 6th Confederate Cav.
GRIFFITH, J. H. F, 14th Inf. Jul. 13, 1864 TN
GRIGSBY, W. L. I, 3rd Inf. Jul. 31, 1863 TN
GRIMES, Josiah L. E, 1st Cav. Feb. 2, 1865 AL
GRIMES, W. J. E, 49th Inf. TN
GROGAN, Anderson. D, 58th Inf. Feb. 12, 1865 NC
GROGAN, Hugh. C, 21st Inf. Feb. 4, 1864 LA
GROSS, Abraham. B, 5th Inf. Dec. 19, 1863 MO
GUINN, Alexander. F, 29th Inf. Jan. 26, 1865 TN
GUINN, Coleman. 53rd Inf. Mar. 5, 1862 TN
GUIST, A. J. G, 1st Cav. TN
GULLEDGE, E. J. K, 36th Inf. Oct. 28, 1864 GA
GUNSON, J. R. I, 9th Inf. Nov. 8, 1864 AR
GUNTE, J. W. C, 4th Inf. Apr. 13, 1862 MS
GUR, Thomas. E, 57th Inf. Jul. 18, 1864 GA

GURNELL, W. S. A, 32nd Inf. May 21, 1863 KY

GUTHRIE, F. H. D, 10th Inf. May 31, 1864 AR

GUTHRIE, J. T. D, 9th Cav. Jun. 15, 1864 TN

GUY, H. S. G, 33rd Inf. May 30, 1864 AL

HACKLER, A. S. I, 28th Cav. MS

HACKLEY, B. H. D, 9th Inf. TX

HAILE, James. F, 30th Inf. Oct. 16, 1863 GA

HAINES, John. C, 1st Butler's Cav. May 15, 1863 KY

HALE, Israel. F, 8th Inf. May 3, 1862 KY

HALE, J. W. Forrest's Cav. Jan. 26, 1864 TN

HALES, J. W. G, 2nd Cav. Oct. 30, 1863 TN

HALL, Alfred. E, 10th Inf. Feb. 1, 1864 KY

HALL, Fielding. E, 10th Inf. Mar. 10, 1864 KY

HALL, J. C. I, 4th Inf. Mar. 17, 1862 MS

HALL, John C. D, 41st Inf. May 3, 1862 TN

HALL, Lee. E, 10th Inf. Mar. 28, 1865 KY

HALL, Samuel. C, 10th Cav. KY

HALL, W. D. H, Hampton's Legion SC

HALLEY, J. B. E, 32nd Inf. Apr. 18, 1862 TN

HALLOWELL, J. D. D, 8th Inf. Mar. 30, 1862 KY

HAM, John. I, 53rd Inf. Apr. 16, 1862 TN

HAMBY, Samuel C. Corput's Co., Lt. Art. Feb. 11, 1865 GA

HAMILTON, A. J. D, 5th Inf. Jul. 17, 1864 KY

HAMILTON, J. B. C, 3rd Cav. Mar. 22, 1864 KY

HAMLET, R. Forrest's Cav. Jun. 30, 1864 TN

HAMLIN, William. D, 29th Inf. Jan. 1, 1864 NC

HAMM, John P. B, 21st Inf. Jul. 24, 1864 AL

HAMMOCK, C. C. B, 19th Dawson's Inf. Jul. 25, 1864 AR

HAMMOND, R. F. C, 25th Inf. Feb. 25, 1864 AR

HAMNER, Johnson. G, 51st Inf. Nov. 17, 1863 AL

HANCOCK, Albert. C, 3rd Inf. Jan. 28, 1864 MO

HANKINS, T. C. I, 26th Inf. Apr. 4, 1862 TN

HANKS, Wiley. Worthington's Bat. Jan. 25, 1864 MS

HANNA, L. A. A, 9th Cav. Jul. 25, 1864 TN

HARDEE, Gilbert W. G, 9th Miller's Cav. Nov. 13, 1864 MS

HARDY, James M. K, 32nd Inf. Feb. 6, 1864 TN

HARLAND, H. F, 2nd Inf. Jul. 21, 1863 TN

HARMS, J. C, Waul's Legion TX

HARPER, J. H. F, 7th Bn. Mar. 4, 1865 MS

HARPER, Jasper. D, 3rd Inf. Jan. 13, 1864 LA

HARRELL, Robert. G, 20th Cav. Feb. 21, 1865 TN
HARRINGTON, W. H. H, 10th Inf. Mar. 23, 1863 MS
HARRIS, Calvin. B, 38th Inf. Apr. 6, 1864 MS
HARRIS, George W. B, 1st Inf. FL
HARRIS, R. B. A, 5th Inf. Dec. 20, 1863 AL
HARRIS, Thomas M. A, 10th Cav. Feb. 11, 1865 KY
HARRISON, Joseph. E, 5th Cav. AR
HARRY, H. A, 63rd Inf. TN
HART, James. B, 2nd Bn. Jan. 17, 1864 MS
HARWELL, Samuel Y. A, 32nd Inf. TN
HARWOOD, John H. D, 64th Inf. Nov. 18, 1863 NC
HAWKINS, R. P. G, 4th Cav. Jan. 11, 1864 GA
HAWKINS, W. P. E, 8th Inf. Mar. 27, 1862 KY
HAYES, Daniel. D, 1st Inf. TX
HAYES, William. F, 32nd Inf. Jun. 15, 1862 TN
HAYS, Isaac. D, 1st Inf. Jan. 31, 1865 GA
HEALEY, Michael. D, Ballentine's Cav. Apr. 10, 1864 MS
HEARD, G. T. D, 31st Inf. Nov. 4, 1864 AR
HEARN, F. A. D, 12th Inf. Oct. 17, 1863 TN
HEDRICK, John S. F, 5th Cav. Dec. 23, 1864 TN
HELMS, A. T. F, 23rd Inf. Mar. 8, 1865 AL
HEMPHILL, William F. A, 9th Inf. Nov. 9, 1863 MS
HENCHEST, James. K, 4th Inf. MS
HENDERSON, Thomas B. A, 3rd Inf. Sep. 13,1863 TN
HENDON, W. J. B, 14th Clark's Inf. TX
HENDRICK, W. H. D, 56th Inf. VA
HANNAGAN, John C. G, 31st Inf. May 1, 1864 LA
HENRY, Lewis. C, 19th Inf. Jan. 19, 1863 MS
HENRY, R. W. 8th Inf. Feb. 28, 1862 KY
HENSLEY, William. D, 1st Inf. Bn. Jun. 1, 1862 TN
HENSON, J. R. K, 53rd Inf. Jun. 21, 1862 TN
HERBERT, Joachin. C, 1st Art. LA
HERBERT, Mertille. C, 1st Art. Jan. 17, 1864 LA
HERNDON, Joseph W. B, 51st Inf. Aug. 2, 1864 AL
HERRIN, Asa. D, 30th Inf. LA
HERRING, B. L. A, 1st Cav. Feb. 6, 1864 LA
HERRING, David L. F, 12th Inf. Dec. 18, 1863 LA
HESTER, J. W. C, 8th Inf. Apr. 20, 1863 TN
HEWITT, R. A. I, 53rd Inf. Sep. 10, 1862 TN
HICKEY, Henry. I, 26th Inf. Jun. 10, 1862 TN

HICKS, Hiram. A, 10th Cav. Mar. 4, 1864 KY

HICKS, Thomas B. D, 1st Inf. TX

HIGGINBOTHAM, A. A. F, 2nd Cav. Jan. 3, 1864 TN

HIGGINS, J. H. A, 4th Inf. May 6, 1862 MS

HIGGINS, J. W. H, 4th Cav. Mar. 2, 1864 GA

HIGH, Albert R. H, 25th Inf. Jan. 9, 1863 LA

HIGHLAND, George. Rivers' Lt. Art. Nov. 28, 1864 AR

HIGHT, Nathaniel. K, 11th Inf. Jan. 14, 1865 MO

HIGHTOWER, William. F, 8th Cav. Feb. 13, 1865 MO

HILL, H. A. E, 4th Inf. Apr. 8, 1862 MS

HILL, John. Forrest's Cav. Jan. 4, 1864 TN

HILTON, J. M. G, 16th Inf. Jan. 13, 1865 TN

HILTON, Rush F. E, 45th Inf. Mar. 2, 1865 VA

HINES, Thomas A. A, 26th Inf. Feb. 25, 1862 TN

HINES, Wiley. H, 12th Inf. Jul. 2, 1863 LA

HINTON, J. W. C, 16th Cav. Bn. Feb. 16, 1865 GA

HIPSHEAR, William. F, 1st Cav. Jul. 31, 1864 TN

HOBUCK, Clifton J. D, 45th Inf. Jan. 20, 1865 VA

HODGES, David. A, 26th Inf. MS

HODGES, David B. 4th Inf. Mar. 4, 1862 MS

HODGES, G. W. G, 8th Cav. Jan. 16, 1865 AR

HOFFMAN, J. D. K, 3rd Inf. Feb. 27, 1864 MS

HOGAN, J. W. A, 4th Inf. Bn. Sep. 5, 1864 AR

HOGAN, James W. B, 62nd Inf. Feb. 7, 1864 NC

HOLBROOK, Hiram. D, 5th Inf. Mar. 5, 1864 KY

HOLDER, J. T. G, 1st Helm's Cav. Mar. 2 1862 KY

HOLLEY, John W. A, 32nd Inf. TN

HOLLOWAY, E. S. A, 1st Inf. Bn. Jan. 30, 1864 LA

HOLLOWAY, T. H. E, 26th Inf. Nov. 13, 1865 TN

HOLLOWELL, Jones W. D, 8th Inf. Mar. 24, 1862 KY

HOLSTON, V. B. B, 36th Inf. VA

HOLT, G. W. A, 1st Inf. Jun. 17, 1864 LA

HOLT, H. C. K, Armistead's Cav. MS

HONEYCUTT, W. F. E, 30th Inf. Mar. 22, 1865 TN

HOPKINS, E. L. I, 30th Inf. Jan. 26, 1862 AR

HOPKINS, George. Lawther's Inf. MO

HOPKINS, J. A. Forrest's Cav. TN

HOPKINS, J. C. B, 12th Inf. Mar. 1, 1864 KY

HOPPER, A. G. C, 32nd Inf. TN

HORLESS, J. M. G, 2nd Inf. Dec. 7, 1863 TN

HORMAN, J. W. D, 45th Inf. Jan. 7, 1865 VA
HORSEY, Thomas H. B, 26th Inf. Mar. 29, 1862 MS
HORTON, A. P. D, 12th Inf. Nov. 30, 1863 MS
HORTON, Andrew. I, 45th Inf. Mar. 5, 1865 VA
HORTON, Louis A. C, 39th Inf. NC
HOSEA, Petts. B, 45th Inf. Jan. 16, 1865 VA
HOUSE, Thomas H. I, 25th Inf. Dec. 23, 1863 AR
HOWARD, Marshall. B, 1st Inf. Bn. Jun. 2, 1862 TN
HOWARD, Pleasant L. A, 4th Inf. Mar. 3, 1862 MS
HOWSLEY, H. P. C, 2nd Mtd. Inf. Jan. 17, 1865 KY
HUBBARD, Harry C. A, 10th Diamond's Cav. Feb. 27, 1865 KY
HUDDLESTON, B. D. K, 3rd Cav. Mar. 16, 1865 TN
HUDSON, J. H. E, 11th Cav. AL
HUFFAKER, R. W. L, 4th Cav. Feb.11, 1865 TN
HUFFMAN, J. D. H, 3rd Inf. Feb. 27, 1864 MS
HUGHES, Green J. I, 3rd Cav. Mar. 27, 1863 AL
HUGHES, I. S. D, Johnston's 1st Inf. Mar. 25, 1862 MS
HUGHES, J. R. H, 9th Cav. TX
HUGHES, W. H. A, 20th Inf. Oct. 25, 1863 MS
HUGHEY, B. A. A, 8th Inf. Mar. 19, 1864 AR
HUIE, W. H. F, 2nd Cav. Oct. 28, 1863 GA
HULL, D. F. E, 10th Inf. Aug. 10, 1864 KY
HULL, Robert. G, 2nd Cav. Aug. 22, 1864 TN
HULSE, William R. E, 60th Inf. Jul. 2, 1863 TN
HUMBLE, John. I, 9th Cav. Sep. 12, 1864 AL
HUMNET, J. B, 51st Inf. Aug. 1, 1863 TN
HUMPHRIES, Jack. K, 18th Inf. SC
HUNT, D. B. I, 2nd Cav. Dec. 16, 1863 MO
HUNT, W. A. B, 27th Inf. Aug. 31, 1863 AL
HUNT, W. C. B, Johnston's 1st Inf. Jul. 30, 1862 MS
HUNTER, Robert. Landis's Bat. Dec. 4, 1863 MO
HURT, Aaron R. C, 36th Inf. Nov. 10, 1864 VA
HURT, W. H. G, 4th Inf. Mar. 2, 1862 MS
HUTCHISON, G. W. H, 36th Inf. Feb. 9, 1865 VA
HUTTO, Joseph. J. F, 53rd Inf. Aug. 7, 1864 AL
HUTZEL, Ezra F. F, 45th Inf. Jan. 29, 1865 VA
IJAMS, B. G. M, 4th Cav. Feb. 26, 1865 AL
IRWIN, S. P. Greer's Inf. Bn. Feb. 24, 1863 TX
IRWIN, William. B, 26th Inf. Dec. 21, 1863 LA
JACKSON, Ethan. D, 12th Cav. KY

JAMES, William H. A, 4th Inf. Mar. 24, 1862 MS
JEATER, W. D. D, 3rd Inf. Jan. 1, 1864 LA
JESSE, Pepper. I, 4th Inf. Apr. 2, 1862 MS
JOHNSON, A. B. A, 14th Inf. KY
JOHNSON, Emmett. G, 45th Inf. Feb. 26, 1865 VA
JOHNSON, J. A. C, 13th Cav. Jun. 22, 1864 TN
JOHNSON, James M. C, 13th Cav. Mar. 13, 1862 TN
JOHNSON, James R. I, 2nd Mtd. Inf. Mar. 20, 1862 KY
JOHNSON, James S. B, 57th Inf. Oct. 17, 1863 AL
JOHNSON, John G. K, 57th Inf. Jan. 28, 1865 AL
JOHNSON, Samuel M. H, 1st Cav. Dec. 14, 1863 MS
JOHNSON, W. T. E, 32nd Inf. Feb. 10, 1864 TN
JOHNSTON, Joseph W. D, 32nd Inf. TN
JONES, C. Signal Corps Feb. 14, 1864
JONES, David. 37th Inf. Nov. 19, 1863 MS
JONES, G. W. G, 1st Cav. MO
JONES, George. C, 26th Inf. Nov. 14, 1863 MS
JONES, Henry. B, 1st Butler's Cav. KY
JONES, Henry H. B, 29th Inf. Sep. 27, 1864 GA
JONES, J. W. B, Walter's Inf. Bn. Dec. 4, 1863 NC
JONES, James. E, 2nd Cav. Mar. 11, 1864 GA
JONES, James G. C, 62nd Inf. Nov. 27, 1863 NC
JONES, Jessie. Forrest's 3rd Cav. TN
JONES, Lucins. D, 3rd Cav. Jul. 11, 1863 TN
JONES, Stephen F. E, 45th Inf. Feb. 15, 1865 VA
JONES, T. A. B, Newton's Cav. Oct. 10, 1864 AR
JONES, Theodore. E, 60th Inf. Oct. 10, 1864 NC
JONES, W. H. A, 4th Inf. Mar. 16, 1862 MS
KEATING, John. G, 13th Inf. Feb. 14, 1865 LA
KEECKER, E. H, 45th Inf. VA
KEITH, D. T. F, 8th Inf. Bn. Jan. 17, 1865 GA
KELLER, Conrad. D, 1st Cav. Aug. 23, 1863 MO
KELLER, J. H. G, 8th Inf. Apr. 4, 1862 KY
KELLEY, Allan K. D, 9th Cav. Aug. 21, 1862 TN
KELLY, L. D. F, 23rd Inf. May 30, 1862 MS
KELLY, Parker. B, 31st Inf. Aug. 19, 1864 TN
KELTNER, E. F. K, 53rd Inf. TN
KEMP, L. G. B, 26th Inf. Apr. 20, 1862 MS
KENNEDY, George W. F, 3rd Inf. Aug. 17, 1862 MS
KEY, George W. D, 5th Cav. Jan. 27, 1865 AL

KEY, J. W. E, 15th Inf. Sep. 26, 1864 TN
KIBBEN, W. H. E, 4th Inf. TX
KIGER, Henry. B, 8th Cav. AR
KILCHRIST, Hickerstan. H, 54th Inf. Jul. 22, 1864 GA
KILLINGSWORTH, Calvin. A, 3rd Cav. Jan. 30, 1864
KIMBALL, William J. D, 2nd Cav. Aug. 29, 1864 MO
KINCAID, J. K. I, 26th Inf. May 2, 1862 TN
KINCAID, T. J. D, 9th Cav. Mar. 7, 1865 TN
KINCAIDE, George W. D, 9th Cav. Feb. 28, 1865 TN
KING, E. H. C, 22nd Inf. May 29, 1864 AL
KING, H. J. E, 26th Inf. Jul. 15, 1862 TN
KING, James H. A, Allison's Cav. TN
KING, John W. H, 60th Inf. Jun. 18, 1863 TN
KING, R. H. I, 41st Inf. Mar. 27, 1862 TN
KING, Robert K. K, 29th Inf. Jan. 31, 1864 NC
KING, S. G, 45th Inf. Aug. 12, 1864 VA
KING, Thomas J. K, 32nd Inf. TN
KING, William. L, 2nd Cav. Jan. 20, 1865 TN
KINNINGHAM, J. S. G, 16th Inf. Dec. 16, 1863 GA
KNOLLE, F. C, Wald's Legion TX
KNOX, George J. F, 5th Inf. Dec. 14, 1865 SC
KOONCE, Daniel M. A, 30th Inf. Aug. 1, 1864 MS
KREECHER, E. H, 45th Inf. Feb. 22, 1865 VA
KUGLE, James M. B, 4th Inf. Mar. 8, 1862 MS
KYLE, Eli. K, 50th Inf. Jul. 4, 1863 TN
LACK, W. G. F, Faulkner's Cav. KY
LADD, John H. B, 8th Mtd. Inf. Mar. 6, 1862 KY
LAFLEUR, Octavo. K, 16th Inf. Apr. 15, 1863 LA
LAIRD, J. P, Moreland's Cav. Sep. 5, 1864 AL
LAKEMAN, F. M. G, 1st Lt. Art. Aug. 19, 1863 MS
LAMBERT, Edward. A, 8th Bn. Horse Art. Feb. 14,1865 LA
LAMBERT, Joseph G. F, 45th Inf. VA
LAMBRIGHT, John M. A, 1st Cav. Feb. 6, 1864 LA
LANCASTER, J. W. A, 60th Inf. Jul. 17, 1863 TN
LAND, E. V. B, 37th Inf. Mar. 28, 1865 MS
LAND, Enoch. G, 2nd Mtd. Rifles AR
LANDERS, John L. A, 60th Inf. VA
LANDRETH, A. J. B, 45th Inf. Mar. 2, 1865 VA
LANDRY, Peirre. B, 1st Horse Art. Nov. 2, 1863 LA
LANE, Thomas. G, 17th Inf. Jan. 30, 1865 TN

LANGLEY, Reuben. C, 1st Inf. Dec. 27, 1864 TN
LARKIS, W. C, 23rd Inf. Jul. 8, 1864 LA
LASAIGNE, Joseph. C, 1st Horse Art. Sep. 16, 1863 LA
LASH, J. W. K, 10th Confederate Cav.
LASHBROOK, S. D. A, 1st Butler's Cav. Feb. 23, 1865 KY
LATAPIE, Pierre. D, 30th Inf. LA
LATHAM, Elias. 41st Inf. Mar. 15, 1863 AL
LAUDERDALE, G. W. F, 12th Cav. Bn. Aug. 30, 1864 TN
LAUDERDALE, J. C. H, 53rd Inf. Nov. 30, 1864 TN
LAW, William. G, 4th Cav. Jan. 28, 1865 AL
LAWRENCE, Thomas. H, 5th Inf. Nov. 26, 1863 MO
LAYTON, George W. G, 40th Inf. Jan. 17, 1865 MS
LEA, James. B, 1st Cav. Mar. 3, 1865 TN
LEBLANC, Trasimond. C, 1st Hvy. Art. Oct. 19, 1863 LA
LEDBETTER, George. D, 5th Cav. Feb. 15, 1865 KY
LEDFORD, Miles M. F, Thomas Legion Dec. 14, 1864 NC
LEE, L. J. K, 41st Inf. Aug. 3, 1862 TN
LEE, O. H. B, 53rd Inf. Aug. 15, 1864 GA
LEE, Richard. Engineer Corps Feb. 9, 1865 AR
LEFAN, James. A, Baxter's Inf. Bn. Mar. 9, 1865 TN
LEJEUNE, Julius. F, 4th Inf. Dec. 21, 1863 LA
LEONARD, P. M. D, 32nd Inf. Mar. 4, 1863 LA
LESLAKER, Frank. Waul's Legion TX
LEWIS, Stephen. Cav. Mar. 15, 1862 TN
LILES, Joseph. H, 41st Inf. May 7, 1862 TN
LILLARD, Augustus M. B, 59th Inf. Nov. 22, 1864 TN
LILLEY, T. J. E, 8th Inf. Jul. 18, 1862 KY
LINDSEY, G. W. A, 26th Inf. MS
LISK, Brannon. I, 60th Inf. Aug. 10, 1863 TN
LITTLE, Daniel. A, 41st Inf. Apr. 15, 1862 TN
LITTLE, John C. D, 51st Inf. Feb. 1, 1864 AL
LITTLE, Swepter. H, 41st Inf. Mar. 22, 1862 TN
LITTLEJOHN, Chester. D, 51st Inf. Feb. 1, 1864 AL
LITTLETON, Sal (Negro Slave). 3rd Inf. MS
LIVELY, Armon D. I, 25th Inf. Mar. 27, 1864 LA
LLOYD, Samuel H. K, 23rd Inf. Mar. 3, 1862 MS
LODEN, Reuben. E, 26th Inf. Mar. 14, 1862 TN
LONG, A. G, 1st Cav. Oct. 28, 1864 TN
LONG, John T. I, 59th Inf. Jul. 15, 1864 TN
LOVE, Joseph. E, 20th Inf. AR

LOVE, Thomas. F, 12th Cav. Bn. Jan. 31, 1865 TN
LOW, Isaac. A, 45th Inf. Mar. 6, 1865 VA
LOWDEN, Thomas. Wilcox's Cav. Mar 1, 1862 KY
LOWERY, J. C. Bowman's Co., Greer's Inf. TX
LOWRY, Newton R. D, 30th Inf. Aug. 25, 1864 AL
LOWRY, R. B. C, 4th Inf. Mar. 13, 1862 MS
LOYD, Samuel H. K, 23rd Inf. Mar. 3, 1862 MS
LUCKETT, D. W. H, 3rd Cav. Nov. 21, 1863 KY
LUMPKINS, Lewis F. D, 32nd Inf. Apr. 14, 1862 TN
LUNSFORD, L. B, Lawton's Cav. AR
LUTTRELL, Hugh. B, 12th Cav. Bn. Feb. 28, 1865 TN
LYONS, J. B, 3rd Inf. Jul. 18, 1863 TN
MABE, William. C, 37th Inf. Sep. 18, 1864 TN
MABEY, F. M. H, 4th Inf. May 3, 1862 MS
MCAFFEE, John. C, 1st Inf. Bn. Apr. 23, 1862 TN
MCALLISTER, J. S., Thompson's Art. VA
MCARVER, James H. C, 40th Inf. Jan. 5, 1865 GA
MCBRIDE, David. G, 45th Inf. Sep. 15, 1864 VA
MCBRIDE, James F. E, 9th Cav. Bn. Apr. 20, 1862 TN
MCBRIDE, Silas H. F, 1st Cav. Jun. 16, 1864 AR
MCCAFFEE, Jasper H. F, 23rd Inf. MS
MCCANLESS, Marshall A. D, 53rd Inf. Sep. 3, 1862 TN
MCCANN, S. L. K, 23rd Inf. Apr. 10, 1862 MS
MCCANTS, P. J. E, 41st Inf. TN
MCCARTER, J. B. A, 1st Inf. MS
MCCARTER, Richard. C, 26th Inf. Mar. 10, 1862 TN
MCCARTY, James. K, 32nd Cav. TN
MCCAULEY, George. D, 3rd Cav. Sep. 24, 1864 MO
MCCAWLEY, George A. D, 1st Inf. Bn. Mar. 17, 1862 TN
MCCLANAHAN, F. R. K, 23rd Inf. Apr. 25, 1862 MS
MCCLARY, William M. B, 53rd Inf. Jun. 21, 1862 TN
MCCLELLAND, J. K. C, 27th Inf. Mar. 10, 1865 VA
MCCLELLAND, Samuel. D, Johnston's 1st Inf. Apr. 9, 1862 MS
MCCLENONS, John T. F, 26th Inf. Feb. 10, 1862 MS
MCCLUNG, Thomas. F, 36th Inf. Feb. 20, 1865 VA
MCCOLLOUGH, R. D, 4th Cav. May 15, 1864 GA
MCCOLLUM, Levi. 2nd Cav. MS
MCCONNELL, Anderson H. E, 53rd Inf. Mar. 10, 1862 TN
MCCONNELL, Arthur C. B, 9th Cav. Aug. 10, 1862 TN
MCCORMICK, George. W, Hughes Cav. Jul. 26, 1862 MO

MCCRAW, W. R. G, 45th Inf. Jan. 4, 1865 VA
MCCROOK, W. L. Bat. Aug. 13, 1863 TN
MCCROW, J. C, 26th Inf. Apr. 2, 1862 MS
MCCULLOUGH, A. M. D, Johnston's 1st Inf. Mar. 16, 1862 MS
MCDERMOTT, John. H, 3rd Inf. FL
MCDONALD, Daniel. B, 21st Inf. Aug. 21, 1863 LA
MCDOUGAL, John. C, Baxter's Cav. Nov. 24, 1863 AL
MCDOWELL, W. L, 1st Cav. Dec. 1, 1863 TN
MCELHANEY, John A. C, 40th Inf. Oct. 17, 1864 AL
MCFALL, Alfred H. E, 2nd Inf. Mar. 29, 1862 KY
MCFARLAND, R. C, 2nd Choctaw
MCFARLAND, W. A. E, 8th Inf. Jan. 13, 1865 MO
MCGEE, John. A, Waul's Legion TX
MCGILL, R. G. D, 12th Cav. Dec. 15, 1864 MS
MCGRADY, John. I, 45th Inf. Dec. 23, 1864 VA
MCINTYRE, William J. D, 32nd Inf. Feb. 2, 1863 AL
MCKEE, Benjamin F. E, 63rd Inf. Sep. 2, 1864 VA
MCKINLEY, J. C. A, 1st Mtd. Rifles Sep. 21, 1864 KY
MCKINNEY, Daniel W. A, 32nd Inf. Mar. 26, 1862 TN
MCKINNEY, M. I, 64th Inf. Feb. 4, 1864 NC
MCKNIGHT, A. J. C, 9th Cav. Aug. 28, 1864 TN
MCLEAN, F. H, 4th Cav. Feb. 10, 1865 AL
MCLERAN, James C. C, 26th Inf. MS
MCLONEY, Aaron. B, 9th Inf. Jun. 20, 1863 KY
MCMAHAN, Pat. A, 1st Butler Cav. Nov. 19, 1863 KY
MCMULLIN, T. N. E, 56th Inf. Dec. 31, 1863 GA
MCMULLIN, Thomas J. E, 56th Inf. Jan. 7, 1864 GA
MCNABB, Jacob. C, 26th Inf. TN
MCNAMARA, James. A, Waul's Legion Sep. 7, 1863 TX
MCNEECE, J. P. C, 53rd Inf. TN
MCNEECE, James. C, 53rd Inf. Apr. 6, 1862 TN
MCNEELY, William. A, 45th Inf. Feb. 4, 1865 VA
MCROSKY, William. Pinkney's Inf. Bn. LA
MALCOMB, Alfred. 4th Inf. MS
MALLORY, Thomas. G, 1st Art. Dec. 16, 1863 MS
MANGAN, Peter. Tobin's Bat. TN
MANGRAM, W. B. B, 30th Inf. TN
MANLEY, Hartwell. E, 32nd Inf. TN
MANN, D. F, 60th Inf. Mar. 1, 1863 NC
MANN, J. B. I, 56th Inf. Jul. 31, 1864 GA

MANSELL, Micajah. F, 16th Inf. Nov. 23, 1864 LA
MANUS, William. B, 38th Inf. May 28, 1864 AL
MARBURGER, G. W. E, Waul's Legion TX
MARIE, Joseph. B, 1st Horse Art. Nov. 10, 1863 LA
MARSH, James. 2nd Bat. Dec. 15, 1863 MO
MARSHALL, Charles. A, Zouave Inf. Bn. Mar. 13, 1864 LA
MARSHALL, J. M. A, 45th Inf. Jan. 31, 1865 VA
MARSHALL, James W. B, 4th Mtd. Inf. Mar. 12, 1862 KY
MARTIN, A. F. I, 1st Inf. TN
MARTIN, Godfrey. A, 1st Inf. Bn. LA
MARTIN, Isaac. G, 9th Cav. AL
MARTIN, J. H. H, 3rd Inf. May 17, 1862 MS
MARTIN, J. P. A, 4th Inf. Jan. 27, 1864 TN
MARTIN, John. 15th Inf. Mar. 9, 1863 LA
MARTIN, John A. C, 39th Inf. NC
MARTIN, M. C, Cav. Apr. 5, 1864 MO
MARTIN, M. C. H, 1st Inf. MS
MARTIN, M. R. K, 4th Inf. Jul. 27, 1862 MS
MARTIN, Martin. H, 1st Cav. Apr. 6, 1864 LA
MARTIN, T. J. H. H, 9th Inf. Oct. 7, 1863 AR
MASON, S. E, 15th Inf. May 13, 1864 TN
MASSA, Lewis. I, 25th Cav. TX
MATHEWS, H. D. H, 41st Inf. Mar. 5, 1862 TN
MATHEWS, Hezekiah. E, 10th Inf. Nov. 10, 1863 TN
MATHEWS, Isom. A, 36th Inf. Nov. 17, 1863 MS
MATHEWS, W. R. C, 16th Cav. TN
MATHIS, J. T. E, 9th Cav. TX
MATTHEWS, G. W. B, 39th Inf. Jan. 29, 1865 MS
MAY, Martin. C, 18th Inf. Jun. 21, 1864 AL
MAY, Thomas. A, 14th Inf. Mar. 3, 1864 LA
MAY, William G. G, 32nd Inf. Apr. 30, 1862 TN
MAYO, Henry (Negro Slave). G, 56th Inf. Mar. 23, 1862 VA
MAYO, J. G. D, 1st Cav. AL
MAYS, Elijah. D, 1st Carnes' Lt. Art. TN
MAYS, T. J. B, Kitchen's Inf. MO
MAYS, William. F, Inf. VA
MEACHUM, J. T. F, Johnston's 1st Inf. MS
MEDLEY, James F. A, Lawther's Inf. Jun. 6, 1864 MO
MEEKS, A. J. 29th Inf. Feb. 27, 1863 MS
MEEKS, Charles. Elliott's Inf. Bn. MO

MELTON, George D. D, 10th Cav. Mar. 25, 1865 MO
MERRILL, W. E, Legion TX
MILES, J. G. C, Mercer's Inf. GA
MILES, J. N. B, 2nd Inf. TN
MILES, John W. B, 2nd Cav. Feb. 17, 1865 KY
MILLER, C. W. I, Hamilton's Legion SC
MILLER, Caleb. D, 10th Diamond's Cav. Aug. 27, 1864 KY
MILLER, G. A. D, Forrest's Scouts Nov. 26, 1863 KY
MILLER, J. B, 79th Inf. Jul. 7, 1863 TN
MILLER, John. D, 3rd Inf. Dec. 12, 1863 MS
MILLER, S. E, 7th Cav. Mar. 24, 1865 MO
MILLER, Thomas E. H, 5th Inf. Jan. 27, 1864 MO
MILLER, William H. E, 26th Inf. Mar. 8, 1862 MS
MILLS, J. M. B, 14th Cav. Mar. 18, 1864 TN
MILNER, John. A, 26th Inf. Mar. 11, 1862 MS
MILSTEAD, F. M. K, 26th Inf. Apr. 27, 1863 AL
MINTCHER, James. K, 4th Inf. Jan. 2, 1865 MS
MINTER, J. F, 1st Inf. TX
MINTER, John N. A, 4th Inf. Mar. 16, 1862 MS
MITCHELL, Daniel. K, 8th Cav. Oct. 30, 1863 TX
MITCHELL, S. H. E, 39th Inf. Nov. 18, 1863 GA
MITCHELL, William D. D, 53rd Inf. Jul. 24, 1862 TN
MIX, C. Foster. F, 4th Inf. Jan. 29, 1864 LA
MIX, John P. K, 2nd Inf. KY
MIZE, John A. H, 15th Inf. Oct. 28, 1863 TN
MOBLEY, Samuel E. E, 1st Cav. FL
MOITRIER, Jean Pierre. A, Zouave Inf. Bn. LA
MONROE, John D. I, 36th Inf. Feb. 10, 1865 MS
MONTGOMERY, B. H, 2nd Inf. Jun. 23, 1862 MS
MONUS, Auguste. A, 23rd Inf. Jun. 30, 1864 LA
MOONEY, A. M. K, 26th Inf. Mar. 22, 1862 MS
MOONEY, Terrence. A, 13th Inf. Dec. 7, 1863 LA
MOORE, Henry. Navy seaman
MOORE, J. B. K, 23rd Inf. MS
MOORE, James. B, Wheelter's Cav. TN
MOORE, James F. C, 26th Inf. Mar. 26, 1862 MS
MOORE, S. T. H, 35th Inf. Oct. 19, 1864 MS
MOORE, T. L. G, 16th Inf. GA
MOORE, Thomas. Tobin's Bat. Nov. 22, 1863 TN
MOORMAN, R. E. L. F, 4th Inf. Mar. 7, 1862 MS

MORASH, Joseph. D, Waul's Legion TX
MORE, Wiley. D, 3rd Inf. Aug. 6, 1863 MS
MORELL, J. S. C, 26th Inf. TN
MORGAN, A. E, 28th Cav. Mar. 5, 1865 MS
MORGAN, J. W, Forrest's Cav. Mar. 30, 1862 KY
MORGAN, John. K, 43rd Inf. Jun. 8, 1863 GA
MORGAN, William A. K, 53rd Inf. Mar. 20, 1864 AL
MORIN, Frank S. D, 4th Cav. KY
MORRIS, Bolen. K, 65th Inf. Aug. 10, 1864 GA
MORRIS, Daniel. A, Davis's Cav. Bn. TN
MORRIS, Edward R. F, 36th Inf. Feb. 26, 1865 VA
MORRIS, J. A. E, 34th Inf. Jul. 28, 1864 GA
MORRIS, Thomas H. D, 1st Inf. Aug. 19, 1862 MS
MORRIS, W. T. H, 30th Inf. Feb. 27, 1864 TN
MORRIS, William. Cobb's Bat. Jun. 23, 1863 KY
MORRISEY, M. Navy landsman Sep. 2, 1864 TN
MORRISON, John. Art. Bat. Feb. 16, 1864 TN
MORROW, J. M. D, Johnston's 1st Inf. Mar. 20, 1862 MS
MOSLEY, Arthur T. D, 12th Inf. Dec. 14, 1863 LA
MOWERY, M. D, 29th Inf. TX
MULLICAN, J. W. D, 16th Inf. May 4, 1863 TN
MULLIGAN, William J. A, 1st Cav. Jul. 24, 1864 KY
MULLINAX, J. S. I, Palmetto Inf. SC
MUNSEY, Harvey. F, 6th Inf. TN
MURPHY, J. W. E, 31st Inf. Aug. 15, 1864 AL
MURPHY, Talton. B, 9th Cav. Mar. 16, 1865 TN
MURRAY, John. A, Green's Bat. LA
MURRAY, L. B, Hawkins' Inf. Sep. 21, 1864 TN
MUSTARD, William D. F, 45th Inf. Feb. 19, 1865 VA
MYERS, Alford A. I, 25th Inf. Feb. 11, 1863 LA
NAGLE, P. E, 1st Inf. TN
NAIL, H. F. A, 1st Cav. Jul. 31, 1854 AL
NAIL, W. W. H, 10th Inf. TX
NEAL, Manuel. I, 4th Inf. MS
NELSON, William. A, 26th Inf. Jun. 12, 1862 TN
NEVILLE, James D. Watson's Bat. Feb. 7, 1864 LA
NEW, Jarrett. D, 42nd Inf. May 14, 1864 GA
NEWELL, Martin. V, Forrest's Cav. Aug. 4, 1864 KY
NEWLAND, William. Navy seaman
NEWMAN, M. H. A, 11th Inf. Feb. 20, 1864 SC

NEWSOM, Jesse T. G, 4th Inf. Apr. 26, 1862 MS
NEWSOME, John. H, 3rd Inf. Apr. 21, 1862 MS
NEWTON, W. H. B, 30th Inf. Jun. 25, 1863 AL
NICHOLAS, W. R. C, 19th Inf. Oct. 20, 1863 LA
NICHOLAS, Wilson. H, Reed's Inf. AR
NICHOLS, Stanley. A, 4th Inf. Bn. Dec. 15, 1863 AR
NICKLES, James. K, 26th Inf. Jul. 20, 1862 TN
NIX, W. H. H, 41st Inf. TN
NIXON, John. C, Burnet's SS TX
NOEL, William. Haldeman's Bat. Art. TX
NOLAN, S. A, 37th Inf. AR
NORRIS, J. W. B, 4th Inf. MS
NORRIS, John. Hutton's Co.; Crescent Art. Jan. 16, 1864 LA
NORRIS, W. T. E, 62nd Inf. TN
NOWLAND, J. W. I, 56th Inf. Jul. 9, 1863 TN
OAKLEY, William A. B, 3rd Cav. Sep. 25, 1864 AL
OAKS, T. M. G, 8th Inf. Mar. 27, 1862 KY
OBERST, C. B, 1st Art. TN
O'BRIANT, Allen. K, 4th Inf. MS
O'BRIEN, Daniel. MS
O'CONNELL, Edward. C, 15th Art. Bn. Dec. 5, 1864 AL
O'GUINN, Coleman F, 53rd Inf. TN
OLIVER, J. D, 29th Inf. Aug. 23, 1863 NC
OLIVER, T. J. H, 1st Inf. TN
ORABAUGH, Gideon A. F, Dec. 10, 1864 VA
ORABAUGH, Samuel. A, 45th Inf. Dec. 10, 1864 VA
OSBORNE, A. A. E, 53rd Inf. Apr. 13, 1862 TN
OUTLAW, David. D, 3rd Cav. Jan. 3, 1864 AL
OVERSTREET, John. C, 7th Inf. Jul. 26, 1864 MS
OWEN, W. M. G, 10th Cav. Feb. 21, 1865 GA
OWENS, A. R. H, 2nd Cav. Jun. 30, 1864 GA
OWENS, James F. B, 4th Inf. Aug. 15, 1862 MS
OWENS, John J. E, 1st Inf. SC
OWENS, R. B. A, 1st Inf. Bn. Jan. 25, 1864 LA
OWENS, R. N. M, 7th Cav. Jan. 23, 1865 AL
OWENS, W. E. A, 15th Inf. Aug. 17, 1864 TN
OZAN, Alfred. A, Zouaves Dec. 6, 1864 LA
PACE, W. S. F, 51st Inf. AL
PAMPLIN, Elijah. D, 53rd Inf. Mar. 7, 1862 TN
PARISH, W. C. Frost's Inf. Oct. 31, 1863 AR

PARK, Andrew J. H, 41st Inf. Mar. 8, 1862 TN
PARK, Jerome. H, 41st Inf. Mar. 26, 1862 TN
PARK, T. J. L. H, 41st Inf. TN
PARKER, A. B. F, 9th Cav. Feb. 28, 1864 TN
PARKER, J. T. D, 62nd Inf. Jun. 12, 1864 NC
PARKER, W. A. Mar. 9, 1862 KY
PARKERSON, G. T. A, 4th Inf. Bn. Jun. 18, 1864 AR
PARRISH, D.F. G, Palmetto SS Aug. 6, 1864 SC
PARROTT, Henry. E, Young's Inf. Bn. Jan. 29, 1864 MO
PARSONS, W. H. D, 58th Inf. Feb. 4, 1865 NC
PARTIN, John L. A, 32nd Inf. Jan. 26, 1865 TN
PATTERSON, B. E. B, 5th Cav. Feb. 21, 1865 TN
PATTERSON, B. F. B, 26th Inf. Mar. 18, 1863 TN
PATTERSON, Jackson. C, 32nd Inf. TN
PATTERSON, William. H, 2nd Cav. Oct.12, 1864 AL
PATTERSON, Y. M. H, 1st Inf. MS
PAYNE, Ira. F, 5th Inf. Jul. 20, 1864 GA
PEARCE, G. W. I, Olmstead's 1st Inf. Feb. 11, 1865 GA
PEARCE, J. M. H, 4th Cav. Jan. 25, 1864 GA
PEARCE, W. W. K, 1st Legion TX
PEARCE, William H. K, 56th Inf. May 21, 1862 VA
PEARSON, S. D. Nelson's Cav. Mar. 17, 1862 GA
PEASY, B.C. A, Davis's Cav. Mar. 5, 1865 VA
PEEL, William. K, 23rd Inf. Mar. 14, 1862 MS
PEGG, William. G, 60th Inf. NC
PEPPER, Jesse. I, 4th Inf. Apr. 2, 1862 MS
PERKINS, Benjamin. E, 56th Inf. Aug. 6, 1862 VA
PERRY, J. H. W. K, 26th Inf. Feb. 6, 1864 AL
PETTIT, Benjamin P. G, 26th Inf. Jul. 9, 1862 MS
PETTS, Hosea. B, 45th Inf. Jan. 16, 1865 VA
PETTY, F. M. I, 11th Cav. Dec. 7, 1863 TN
PETTY, George R. A, 1st Inf. Bn. TN
PETTY, Jasper N. H, 37th Shaler's Inf. AR
PHELPS, Ephraim. A, 41st Inf. Mar. 20, 1862 TN
PHILLIPS, David B. C, 32nd Inf. May 10, 1862 TN
PHILLIPS, E. H. A, 1st Inf. Bn. Jan. 20, 1864 LA
PHILLIPS, J. F. A, 63rd Inf. Nov. 12, 1864 GA
PHILLIPS, John. L, 10th Bat. Aug. 10, 1864 KY
PHILLIPS, Nathan. G, 58th Inf. Aug. 7, 1864 NC
PHILLIPS, R. J. E, 4th Inf. Bn. Sep. 29, 1864 LA

PHILPOT, J. A. F, 41st Inf. Mar. 2, 1862 TN
PICKEN, John. C, Forrest's Cav. Dec. 23, 1863 AL
PICKENS, J. P. E, 26th Inf. Mar. 20, 1862 MS
PIERCE, Joseph. I, 58th Inf. Aug. 8, 1864 NC
PIERCY, Charles. G, 23rd Inf. May 7, 1864 AR
PIERSON, James. A, 3rd Inf. MS
PINKSTON, John. K, 26th Inf. Feb. 25, 1862 MS
PIRKLE, L. F. H, 7th Cav. Jul. 21, 1864 AL
PIRTLE, J. H. D, 2nd Mtd. Rifles AR
PLUNK, James M. I, 1st Cav. Jan. 29, 1864 MS
PLYER, J. A, 9th Inf. Nov. 30, 1864 AL
POE, James R. A, 9th Cav. Aug. 18, 1864 AL
POLLARD, Joseph. D, 18th Cav. Jan. 25, 1865 VA
POLLOCK, John. C, 18th Inf. Mar. 13, 1865 TN
PONDER, Levi C. I, 61st Inf. Dec. 31, 1864 AL
POOR, James M. E, 38th Inf. Dec. 8, 1863 TN
PORTER, Andrew J. K, 5th Inf. TN
PORTER, C. C. G, Dobbin's Inf. AR
PORTER, William H. A, 8th Inf. Jan. 14, 1864 MO
POSEY, John W. I, 37th Inf. Feb. 20, 1865 MS
POSTON, Archibald. Bell's Inf. AR
POTTS, Elza. A, 20th Inf. May 14, 1864 GA
POUND, C. C. 10th Inf. Jan. 17, 1864 MO
POWELL, Daniel. H, 46th Inf. Jan. 26, 1864 GA
POWERS, John. E, 16th Inf. Apr. 11, 1863 LA
PREWITT, John S. A, 31st Inf. Jun. 30, 1863 AL
PRICE, Samuel W. B, 27th Cav. Bn. Aug. 31, 1864 VA
PRICE, William. Forrest's Cav. Jan. 10, 1864 KY
PRIDGEN, J. T. E, 19th Inf. Jun. 11, 1864 AL
PRITCHARD, J. P. K, 12th Cav. Jan. 22, 1865 KY
PROVINCE, S. L. H, 1st Inf. Mar. 29, 1862 MS
PRYTON, H. D, 9th Inf. Aug. 28, 1862 TN
PURSER, J. W. K, 4th Inf. Mar. 15, 1862 MS
QUILL, J. N. F, 46th Inf. Aug. 3, 1864 TX
RAGSDALE, John. A, 8th Inf MO
RAHN, E. W. G, Olmstead's 1st Inf. GA
RAINEY, J. C. I, 13th Inf. TN
RAINEY, Robert. H, McGehee's Inf. Mar. 7, 1865 AR
RALER, R. V. G, 19th Inf. TN
RAND, P. C. Navy seaman

RANDOLPH, William. G, 26th Inf. Mar. 23, 1862 MS
RANKIN, David. H, 5th Cav. TN
RAVER, Isaac M. M. B, 30th Inf. Jul. 30, 1863 AL
RAY, General. G, 4th Inf. TN
RAY, J. P. M. K, 4th Inf. MS
RAY, Porter T. K, 4th Inf. Mar. 21, 1862 MS
RAYNOR, J. B. G, 3rd Inf. AL
READ, J. B. D, 25th Inf. May 1, 1863 AL
READ, Noe F. 6th Inf. Jun. 18, 1862 TN
REARDEN, Thomas.
REDD, D. F. D, Newman's Cav. AL
REDDING, James D. F, 29th Inf. Oct. 6, 1863 GA
REDSLEEVE, J. G. C, Thomas's Legion Feb. 2, 1865 NC
REECE, W. H. C, 51st PR. Jan. 1, 1864 AL
REED, John. A, 4th Cav. Dec. 15, 1863 TN
REED, P. A. A, 4th Inf. Dec. 29, 1864 TN
REED, Thomas. E, 1st Lt. Art. Dec. 25, 1863 MS
REED, W. M. B. E, 51st Inf. Mar. 28, 1864 AL
REESE, G. B, 3rd Inf. Jan. 15, 1865 GA
REEVES, H. D. E, 30th Inf. Jun. 12, 1864 LA
REGAN, F. S. A, 1st Inf. Bn. LA
REMINGTON, Moses L. K, 4th Inf. Aug. 25, 1863 KY
REPASS, Henry L. B, 45th Inf. Aug. 22, 1864 VA
REYNOLDS, George. F, 27th Inf. Aug. 31, 1864 VA
RHINEHART, William G. C, 62nd Inf. Mar. 18, 1864 NC
RHOTON, Tolbert. C, 45th Inf. Nov. 26, 1864 VA
RICE, Harry. Hoskin's Bat., Lt. Art. Jan. 7, 1865 MS
RICE, James L. H, 58th Inf. Aug. 26, 1864 NC
RICE, Reuben. C, Coffee's Cav. Jan. 13, 1865 MO
RICE, Thomas L. K, 3rd Inf. Aug. 7, 1863 TN
RICHARD, Frank. C, Coffee's Cav. Mar. 5, 1865 MO
RICHARDS, Eli C. H, 4th Inf. Mar. 4, 1862 TN
RICHARDSON, M. B. A, 4th Cav. Jul. 19, 1864 GA
RICHARDSON, Robert T. I, 56th Inf. Mar. 31, 1862 VA
RICHEY, John. C, 41st Inf. Mar. 7, 1863 AL
RIDDLE, Charles M. H, 26th Inf. MS
RIDGWAY, James J. C, 6th Inf. Jul. 30, 1863 MO
RIKARD, Charles. E, Johnston's 1st Inf. Mar. 16, 1862 MS
RILEY, William. B, 36th Inf. MS
ROBERT, Agrippa. G, 4th Inf. MS

ROBERTS, A. P. B, 4th Inf. Apr. 26, 1862 MS
ROBERTS, Caleb D. D, 5th Mtd. Inf. May 8, 1865 KY
ROBERTS, James. D, 5th Mtd. Inf. KY
ROBERTS, N. W. I, 37th Inf. Feb. 28, 1865 TN
ROBERTS, Reuben J. A, 54th Inf. Jul. 26, 1864 GA
ROBERTSON, Sanford. B, 5th Cav. Apr. 10, 1864 KY
ROBINSON, A. J. G, 28th Cav. MS
ROBINSON, J. M. C. K, 26th Inf. Mar. 14, 1862 MS
ROBINSON, John T. I, 41st Inf. Mar. 15, 1862 TN
ROBINSON, Robert L. G, 2nd Duke's Cav. Dec. 21, 1864 KY
ROBINSON, William. H, Hampton's Legion SC
ROBINSON, William M. H, 27th Inf. Jul. 20, 1864 VA
RODEN, A. C. I, 32nd Inf. TN
RODGERS, A. W. Ward's Bn., Lt. Art. Mar. 6, 1865 AL
RODGERS, Martin R. H, 2nd Inf. Nov. 2, 1863 TX
RODRY, J. B. C, 28th Cav. Aug. 5, 1864 MS
ROGERS, B. H. C, 26th Inf. Mar. 20, 1862 MS
ROGERS, Mark. H, Ashby's 2nd Cav. TN
ROLLINS, W. F. I, 16th Inf. LA
ROSENTHAL, P. English's Co., Lt. Art. Nov. 15, 1863 MS
ROWLAND, J. R. Mar. 5, 1863
RUDIGER, A. English's Co., Lt. Art. MS
RUNION, S. O. B, 26th Inf. Jul. 21, 1862 TN
RUSSELL, A. J. A, 58th Inf. Jul. 22, 1864 AL
RUSSELL, John R. H, 4th Inf. Mar. 4, 1862 MS
RUSSELL, Samuel R. B, 61st Inf. Aug. 27, 1863 TN
RUTH, M. L. C, 32nd Inf. TN
RUTH, S. D. C, 32nd Inf. Apr. 21, 1862 TN
RUTLEDGE, Martin. H, 23rd Inf. Aug. 14, 1864 VA
RYALS, J. G. B, 4th Inf. MS
RYAN, James. D, 13th Inf. Mar. 1, 1863 LA
RYKARD, J. D. K, 62nd Inf. Dec. 16, 1863 NC
ST. CLAIR, James. B, 3rd Inf. Sep. 16, 1863 MS
SAMPLE, W. A. G, 4th Inf. May 20, 1862 MS
SAMS, J. L. D, 29th Inf. Jan. 6, 1864 NC
SASCON, W. E. 41st Inf. Sep. 5, 1863 AL
SAUNDERS, W. T. D, 1st Inf. Jun. 26, 1862 MS
SAVILLS, James. D, 8th Inf. KY
SAWYERS, Samuel. H, 51st Inf. Jul. 5, 1864 GA
SAYERS, Richard L. C, 63rd Inf. Mar. 10, 1865 VA

SCALES, J. C. G, 51st Cav. Dec. 17, 1863 AL
SCALLIEN, Alcide. I, 1st Art. Jan. 14, 1864 LA
SCHMITT, Frederick. D, 28th Thomas's Inf. Sep. 12, 1863 LA
SCHNEIDER, J. M. F, 36th Inf. VA
SCOTT, James H. D, 1st Mtd. Rifles Aug. 19, 1864 KY
SCOTT, Jette H. K, 1st Cav. Feb. 11, 1865 AR
SCOTT, John M. A, 42nd Inf. Jan. 15, 1865 GA
SCRITCHFIELD, S. B. B, 4th Cav. Dec. 17, 1863 GA
SCRUGGS, John A. D, 61st Inf. Jul. 9, 1863 TN
SCRUGGS, R. M. E, 16th Cav. Nov. 14, 1864 TN
SEABORN, J. B. A, 62nd Inf. May 10, 1864 TN
SELLERS, Isaac. G, 41st Inf. May 7, 1862 TN
SELLERS, James H. D, 4th Cav. Feb. 1, 1865 KY
SELLERS, N. M. B, 5th Inf. Dec. 28, 1863 TN
SELLINGER, J. L. C, 41st Inf. Feb. 22, 1863 MS
SEMPLE, John T. C, 1st Cav. Jan. 12, 1864 LA
SERGEANT, Elijah. Fuller's Bat. Dec. 16, 1863 LA
SHADWICK, Benjamin. 1st Bat. MO
SHAPPELL, T. D. A, 2nd Inf. Mar. 31, 1864 MO
SHARP, John M. A, Stuart's Inf. Bn. Feb. 20, 1865 AL
SHAW, Benjamin F. F, 20th Inf. TX
SHAW, R. P. G, 48th Inf. Oct. 10, 1864 TN
SHELTON, E. H. B, 20th Inf. Sep. 2, 1864 TN
SHELTON, George R. I, 32nd Inf. Feb. 2, 1863 AL
SHERWOOD, W. H. G, 1st Cav. Dec. 30, 1863 MO
SHIELDS, R. O. K, 1st Inf. Apr. 30, 1862 MS
SHIELDS, Samuel. C, 45th Inf. Feb. 8, 1865 VA
SHORT, Lewis. I, Washington Inf. Jan. 9, 1865 TN
SHORTER, C. C. G, 37th Inf. Mar. 22, 1865 VA
SHRADER, William. D, 45th Inf. Mar. 22, 1865 VA
SHULTZ, M. V. I, 3rd Cav. Mar. 5, 1864 TN
SHUMBERGER, J. W. A, 9th Cav. Feb. 20, 1864 MS
SIDDON, John I. B, 2nd Inf. MS
SIMMONS, M. L. G, 39th Inf. GA
SIMMONS, W. T. E, 1st Inf. Jul. 27, 1864 TN
SIMMONS, William R. D, 60th Inf. Feb. 27, 1865 VA
SIMMS, David. E, 1st Cav. Jan. 25, 1865 MS
SIMPSON, C. C. H, 4th Cav. Feb. 10, 1865 AL
SIMPSON, M. Street's Inf. Bn. MS
SINGLE, James. C, Walker's Inf. Bn. NC

SINGLETON, Francis. C, 1st Cav. Mar. 20, 1864 LA
SINON, John. G, 4th Inf. GA
SIPES, Abraham. A, 11th Inf. Sep. 14, 1863 TN
SISK, Branson. I, 60th Inf. TN
SKINNER, A. W. A, 12th Inf. TN
SLATE, Giles B. E, 56th Inf. May 4, 1862 VA
SLATER, John W. I, 29th Cav. TX
SLOAN, Henry T. E, 10th Inf. Jul. 29, 1864 KY
SLOAN, Jasper. F, 10th Cav. Jul. 30, 1864 KY
SMITH, D. G. B, 1st ST. Inf. LA
SMITH, G. W. C, 4th Inf. MS
SMITH, George. 15th Inf. May 13, 1863 LA
SMITH, George W. F, 36th Inf. Dec. 5, 1864 VA
SMITH, H. A. F, 3rd Cav. Jan. 4, 1865 KY
SMITH, H. L. N. B, 4th Inf. Mar. 26, 1862 MS
SMITH, Henry. Colms' Inf. Bn. Mar. 30, 1862 TN
SMITH, Henry. A, 1st Inf. Bn. TN
SMITH, J. A. C, 21st Cav. Mar. 6, 1865 VA
SMITH, J. B. D, 61st Inf. Jan. 25, 1865 TN
SMITH, J. M. B, 32nd Inf. TN
SMITH, J. R. E, 25th Inf. LA
SMITH, James. I, 45th Inf. Sep. 13, 1864 VA
SMITH, John. G, 2nd Inf. TX
SMITH, Joseph. I, 1st Confederate Bn.
SMITH, Joseph P. A, 42nd Inf. Aug. 20, 1863 AL
SMITH, L. H. A, 9th Cav. Feb. 9, 1865 AL
SMITH, M. D. A, 1st Inf. Bn. Mar. 7, 1862 TN
SMITH, P. E. Conscript TN
SMITH, R. A. K, Armistead's Inf. Jan. 25, 1865 MS
SMITH, Robert J. F, 53rd Inf. Mar. 12, 1862 TN
SMITH, Samuel. D, 1st Inf. Mar. 12, 1862 TN
SMITH, Sanford. I, 7th Inf. Feb. 18, 1865 GA
SMITH, Seaborn. E, 4th Russell's Cav. Feb. 16, 1864 AL
SMITH, W. C. B, 1st Bn. Mtd. Rifles Mar. 28, 1864 KY
SMITH, William B. I, 6th Cav. TX
SMITHY, John. B, Shelby's Cav. Jun. 29, 1864 MO
SMOOT, James. K, 25th Inf. Sep. 8, 1863 LA
SNELL, C. H. H, 1st Inf. FL
SNELSON, J. W. W. C, 4th Inf. Mar. 18, 1862 MS
SNELSON, W. B. C, 29th Inf. Mar. 18, 1862 MS

SNIDER, John W. C, 62nd Inf. Dec. 2, 1863 NC
SOLIS, Adolphe. C, 28th Thomas's Inf. Jan. 10, 1864 LA
SPAULDING, Martin E. A, 2nd Inf. Mar. 26, 1864 MO
SPEARS, Alfred. K, 45th Inf. Dec. 10, 1864 VA
SPENCE, S. L. D, 15th Inf. Jul. 30, 1864 AL
SPIDER, John W. C, 62nd Inf. Dec. 2, 1863 NC
SPRACHER, Levi. G, 45th Inf. Feb. 25, 1865 VA
SPRAY, W. L. D, 41st Inf. May 5, 1862 TN
SPROLES, J. C, 4th Inf. MS
SPROLES, Spencer S. G, 4th Inf. Mar. 28, 1862 MS
SQUIRES, M. W. C, 3rd Inf. Mar. 6, 1864 LA
STAFFORD, Adam F. I, 36th Inf. VA
STAFFORD, M. E, 4th Inf. MS
STAFFORD, Wyatt P. I, 36th Inf. Mar. 30, 1865 VA
STAINBACK, Robert. E, 56th Inf. Apr. 25, 1862 VA
STANDFORD, Malcomb. 4th Inf. Feb. 27, 1862 MS
STANFORD, W. W. C, 11th Cav. AL
STAPLES, John M. E, 2nd Cav. MD
STARK, F. H. I, 5th Inf. Feb. 23, 1863 AR
STARK, W. F. I, Gordon's 1st Cav. Nov. 26, 1863 MO
STARKE, James C. F, 8th Cav. Jan. 12, 1864 AR
STARLING, Andrew. C, 45th Inf. Feb. 11, 1865 VA
STATON, Peter. E, 45th Inf. Oct. 26, 1864 VA
STATTERY, Thomas. E, 10th Inf. TN
STEAKLEY, Pinckney. E, 1st Inf. Bn. May 12, 1862 TN
STECK, A. C, Waul's Legion TX
STEPHENS, T. J. I, 32nd Inf. TN
STEPP, John A. H, 16th Inf. Nov. 28, 1863 TN
STEVENS, A. T. F, Harrison's Bat. Feb. 20, 1864 LA
STEVENS, G.B. B, Mercer's Inf. Bn. AR
STEVENSON, Bradley. D, 1st Inf. GA
STEVENSON, H. H. G, 17th Inf. Feb. 22, 1864 LA
STEWARD, Michael. H, 56th Inf. Mar. 24, 1862 VA
STEWART, Jasper. G, 16th Inf. Jan. 14, 1864 GA
STEWART, Matthew. K, 2nd Inf. Bn. Nov. 10, 1863 MO
STIDHAM, J. M. F, 25th Inf. Mar. 8, 1865 AL
STILLWELL, L. Baldwin Corput's Co., Lt. Art. Jan. 17, 1865 GA
STINSON, John. A, 34th Inf. Feb. 5, 1865 MS
STOLL, George. B, 3rd Inf. Mar. 11, 1864 MS
STONE, William. 10th Inf. Feb. 11, 1865 KY

STORY, Enoch. K, 18th Inf. Jan. 27, 1865 AL
STOVALL, Lumpkin. I, 26th Inf. MS
STRACNER, Hugston. H, 30th Inf. Jul. 8, 1864 AL
STRADER, John L. A, 30th Inf. Jun. 30, 1863 AL
STROUSS, George W. D, Olmstead's 1st Inf. GA
STUBBLEFIELD, B. D. H, 29th Inf. Feb. 17, 1865 TX
STUKES, G. W. Cameron's Co., ST. MS
STURDIVENT, W. O. C, 8th Cav. Feb. 28, 1864 AR
SUGG, C. A. D, 3rd Bn. ST. MS
SULLIVAN, John. B, 32nd AL Feb. 11, 1864 AL
SULT, John. B, 45th Inf. Jan. 2, 1865 VA
SUMMERS, Jasper. K, 9th Inf. Mar. 26, 1864 MO
SUMPTER, G. L, 1st Cav. Dec. 19, 1864 TN
SWAN, H. C. E, 6th Cav. Nov. 26, 1863 KY
SWEARINGEN, James. B, 28th Inf. Dec. 15, 1864 TN
SWEETEN, Levi. C, 25th Inf. Sep. 11, 1863 AR
SWINGLE, H. F. D, Johnston's 10th Cav. Dec. 19, 1864 KY
SYRILLE, Jex. G, 28th Inf. LA
TABER, E. E, 64th Inf. Jan. 4, 1864 NC
TABLER, Aaron. I, 45th Inf. VA
TALLEY, Irwin. M, 31st Inf. Sep. 19, 1863 AR
TALLEY, John S. A, 18th Inf. Nov. 14, 1863 TN
TATE, C. C. K, 59th Inf. Dec. 2, 1863 TN
TAYLOR, Benjamin F. I, 2nd Inf. Mar. 12, 1862 KY
TAYLOR, F. H. F, 3rd Bat. Dec. 2, 1863 KY
TAYLOR, Harold. C, 45th Inf. Mar. 6, 1865 VA
TAYLOR, Isaac A. B, 56th Inf. Mar. 11, 1862 VA
TAYLOR, J. G. D, 6th Cav. Jan. 21, 1865 AL
TAYLOR, James A. I, 2nd Inf. Aug. 14, 1864 MO
TAYLOR, James E. B, 1st Inf. Bn. Mar. 29, 1862 TN
TAYLOR, John. E, 8th Inf. Feb. 16, 1865 TN
TAYLOR, Milburn. 4th Inf. Mar. 3, 1862 MS
TAYLOR, William. E, 4th Inf. Jul. 20, 1864 MO
TEAR, T. T. B, 4th Inf. MS
TEEMS, William J. D, Johnston's 1st Inf. Apr. 8, 1862 MS
TEETERS, Sylvester. F, 5th Mtd. Inf. KY
TEETERS, Walsey. D, 5th Inf. KY
TENNISON, R. F. A, 26th Inf. Mar. 23, 1862 MS
TERRELL, John D. I, 4th Inf. MS
TERRY, J. H. B, 26th Inf. MS

TEW, Peter. D, Crandall's Inf. Dec. 22, 1864 AR
THOMAS, S. I, 33rd Inf. Feb. 24, 1864 TN
THOMAS, Samuel. B, 25th Inf. Aug. 17, 1863 LA
THOMAS, W. S. H, 16th Inf. Aug. 17, 1863 AL
THOMAS, William. C, McGehee's Inf. Feb. 26, 1865 AR
THOMASTON, W. M. G, 4th Inf. Mar. 20, 1862 MS
THOMPSON, John R. B, Kitchen's Cav. Mar. 18, 1865 AR
THOMPSON, T. S. B, 1st Inf. Bn. TN
THOMPSON, Wilbur G, 59th Inf. Aug. 12, 1864 GA
THOMPSON, William H. G, 27th Cav. Bn. Mar. 3, 1864 VA
THRASHER, J. P. H, McGehee's Inf. Jan.30, 1865 AR
TIMMONS, E. H. A, 8th Inf. KY
TODD, W. A. A, 4th Inf. Apr.15, 1862 MS
TOLAND, J. W. H, 26th Inf. Mar. 30, 1862 MS
TOMBERLIN, J. E. F, 62nd Inf. Oct. 21, 1863 NC
TOWNSEND, A. P. E, 4th Inf. MS
TOWNSON, Robert. E, 4th Inf. MS
TRACEY, A. W. L, 6th Mtd. Inf. May 5, 1864 KY
TRAMEL, Joshua C. B, Allison's Cav. TN
TRAVIS, W. C. A, 26th Inf. Mar. 6, 1862 MS
TREVEY, J. J. H, 14th Cav. Feb. 9, 1865 VA
TRIBLE, E. J. C, 9th Inf. Apr. 9, 1864 MO
TRIPLETT, E. W. H, 29th Inf. Jul. 31, 1864 NC
TRUSSLER, John L. B, Cav. Aug. 25, 1864 VA
TUCKER, J. W. Grave's Bat. Apr. 12, 1862 KY
TUNSTALL, E. H. I, 28th Cav. Nov. 16, 1863 MS
TURLEY, Solomon. B, 45th Inf. VA
TURNER. 4th Inf. Mar. 8, 1862 MS
TURNER, J. E. K, 51st Inf. Jun. 12, 1862 TN
TUTTLE, Francis M. E, 5th Cav. Feb. 6, 1865 MO
TUTTLE, John. B, 3rd Inf. Dec. 20, 1863 MS
VADEN, Robert. I, 7th Cav. MO
VALDEWAIRE, Clestin. I, 13th Inf. Mar. 28, 1864 LA
VAN HUSS, Valentine. H, 27th Cav. Bn. Aug. 22, 1864 VA
VANCE, William C. I, 10th Diamond's Cav. Dec. 22, 1864 KY
VANDRIVERS, S. W. H, 32nd Inf. Dec. 21, 1864 AL
VANPELT, John. B, 2nd Inf. Aug. 13, 1864 TN
VANWAY, Jacob. Humphrey's Co., Lt. Art. Nov. 20, 1863 AR
VARNEY, M. B. B, 45th Inf. Bn. Apr. 2, 1865 VA
VASSER, Robert. G, 9th Inf. Jan. 16, 1864 MO

VAUGHN, Sion. D, 45th Inf. Aug. 19, 1864 VA
VEASEY, A. J. A, 11th Inf. AR
VERTREES, Joseph. St. Louis Bat. Jun. 1, 1864 MO
VICKERS, Jackson. F, 3rd Cav. Jan. 27, 1865 MO
VICROY, John. E, Freeman's Art. TN
VINES, M. L. A, Harper's Cav. VA
VINYARD, Noah H. D, 37th Inf. Oct. 21, 1863 TN
VIRGELY, Barney. B, 8th Inf. Sep. 1, 1863 GA
WAGNER, J. M. F, 1st Cav. Feb. 28, 1865 TN
WALKER, J. W. C, 4th Inf. Apr. 13, 1862 MS
WALKER, James. H. E, 32nd Inf. Feb. 7, 1865 AR
WALKER, William J. B, 38th Inf. Feb. 3, 1865 AL
WALLACE, Lucas. C, 19th Inf. LA
WARD, E. G. K, 43rd Inf. Nov. 26, 1863 TN
WARD, Thomas D. K, 42nd Inf. Mar. 7, 1862 TN
WARD, Thomas G. B, Olmstead's 1st Inf. Mar. 27, 1865 GA
WARDEN, W. R. A, 41st Inf. TN
WARREN, J. W. A, Colms' 1st Inf. Bn. Aug. 7, 1862 TN
WARREN, John. F, 4th Inf. Bn. Dec. 28, 1863 LA
WARREN, Thomas. A, 41st Inf. TN
WATSON, Cornelius. K, Wood's Cav. MO
WATSON, L. R. F, 8th Cav. TX
WEAVER, Felix C. C, 21st Cav. Oct. 13, 1864 VA
WEBB, Granville. I, 45th Inf. Aug. 15, 1864 VA
WEBB, Jesse. H, 3rd Inf. TN
WEEMS, Andy. D, 10th Cav. Nov. 24, 1863 AL
WELDEN, A. J. Mar. 5, 1862 TN
WELLS, Barney. E, 4th Cav. Jan. 25, 1865 KY
WELLS, J. J. B, 32nd Inf. Aug. 3, 1864 TN
WELLS, J. M. F, 23rd Inf. Aug. 25, 1862 MS
WELLS, James E. Scoggin's Bat. Nov. 30, 1864 GA
WELLS, M. E. F, 3rd Inf. Apr. 9, 1862 MS
WEMINS, Jacob. A, 20th Inf. Mar. 1, 1863 LA
WESLICK, Calvin. I, 27th Cav. Bn. Dec. 5, 1864 VA
WEST, Jeffrey. E, 26th Inf. Jan. 3, 1864 TN
WEST, M. N. 31st Inf. Jan. 27, 1864 LA
WEST, Pincey C. A, 31st Inf. May 11, 1864 LA
WESTBROOKS, Hezekiah G. B, 7th Inf. Oct. 10, 1863 KY
WESTMORELAND, L. D. I, Holcombe's Legion SC
WHITAKER, Joseph L. 2nd Inf. TX

WHITE, C. F. B, 4th Inf. MS
WHITE, D. M. A, 1st Horse Art. Feb. 14, 1864 TN
WHITE, J. H. K, 8th Inf. Dec. 10, 1864 VA
WHITE, James D. G, 2nd Mtd. Cav. May 17, 1862 KY
WHITE, Joseph. A, 8th Cav. Feb. 23, 1865 KY
WHITE, M. W. D, 42nd Inf. Feb. 24, 1865 AL
WHITEHEAD, A. H. K, 1st Lt. Art. Mar. 17, 1864 MS
WHITLEY, J. C, Allison's Cav. TN
WHITT, John. E, 2nd Inf. Mar. 31, 1862 KY
WHITWORTH, A. M. B, 44th Cav. TN
WICKHAM, Robert D. C, 36th Inf. Oct. 26, 1864 VA
WICKS, A. A. D, 41st Inf. Apr. 20, 1862 TN
WICKS, J. W. D, 41st Inf. Mar. 29, 1862 TN
WILBURN, Isaac. C, Hampton's Legion SC
WILKERSON, Columbus. A, 15th Inf. Mar. 26, 1864 AR
WILKINSON, B. B, 15th Inf. Jan. 4, 1864 AR
WILLETT, James A. A, 33rd Inf. Dec. 10, 1863 AL
WILLETT, Simeon. D, Hawkins' Cav. MO
WILLIAMS, Andrew J. D, 53rd Inf. Mar. 26, 1862 TN
WILLIAMS, H. C. K, 21st Inf. TX
WILLIAMS, Isam. I, 60th Inf. Dec. 28, 1863 TN
WILLIAMS, John. D, 6th Cav. Feb. 13, 1865 KY
WILLIAMS, Jonathan. E, 45th Inf. Aug. 24, 1864 VA
WILLIAMS, Joseph W. C, 4th Inf. Mar.1, 1862 MO
WILLIAMS, N. E. I, 3rd Cav. Jan. 7, 1865 GA
WILLIAMS, Reuben R. D, 8th Mtd. Inf. Jun. 20, 1862 KY
WILLIAMS, Robert T. I, 9th Cav. TX
WILLIAMS, Thomas. K, 8th Cav. Jan. 22, 1865 TX
WILLIAMS, W. O. A, 4th Inf. Mar. 17, 1862 MS
WILLIN, B. A, 3rd Confederate
WILLKERSON, James. E, 2nd Cherokee
WILSON, G. D. A, 8th Inf. Jul. 26, 1864 TN
WILSON, George. E, Olmstead's 1st Inf. Nov. 30, 1864 GA
WILSON, George. P, Forrest's Cav. Mar. 5, 1862 KY
WILSON, Jesse P. H, 60th Inf. Feb. 11, 1865 VA
WILSON, S. L. E, 13th Cav. Dec. 12, 1863 TN
WILTSHIRE, Henry. C, 4th Inf. May 11, 1862 MS
WINCHESTER, William. E, 29th Inf. Jan. 28, 1864 NC
WINDSOR, S. E. A, 1st Cav. Dec. 19, 1863 LA
WINFREY, J. M. E, 35th Inf. Jul. 31, 1864 AL

WINTER, Fred. B, 1st Bn. Waul's Legion TX
WISELY, Joel S. B, 45th Inf. Feb. 20, 1865 VA
WOMACK, John C. H, 26th Inf. May 26, 1862 MS
WOOD, Bryant. A, 54th Inf. Jul. 26, 1864 GA
WOOD, Daniel. A, 54th Inf. Jul. 24, 1864 GA
WOODRUFF, James H. C, 1st Cav. Dec. 16, 1863 LA
WOODS, G. J. I, 45th Inf. Jul. 30, 1864 VA
WOODYARD, James. I, 36th Inf. Mar. 8, 1865 VA
WOODYARD, Joseph G. I, 36th Inf. Aug. 6, 1864 VA
WREN, Jasper. A, 12th Inf. Feb. 26, 1864 LA
WRENN, F. T. A, 26th Inf. Mar. 10, 1862 MS
WRIGHT, Albert J. B, 56th Inf. Mar. 17, 1862 VA
WRIGHT, Franklin G. D, 14th Cav. Aug. 17, 1863 TX
WRIGHT, G. W. K, Thomas's Legion Mar. 10, 1865 NC
WRIGHT, J. B. C, 41st Inf. Apr. 5, 1862 TN
WRIGHT, James C. K, 5th Cav. Jul. 15, 1864 TN
WRIGHT, W. O. C, 26th Inf. Mar. 14, 1862 MS
WULFINGER, John. B, Zouave Inf. Bn. Jan. 4, 1864 LA
WYATT, Riley B. I, 36th Inf. MS
WYATT, W. H. Cooper's Inf. TX
WYDNER, P. D, 63rd Inf. VA
WYLER, Martin L. C, 1st Inf. Apr. 26, 1862 MS
WYNN, B. A. F, 26th Inf. Aug. 6, 1862 MS
YARBERRY, O. L. K, 22nd Inf. SC
YEADON, J. P. F, 1st Cav. TN
YEAGER, W. F. I, 18th Inf. Jul. 31, 1864 AL
YEAGER, William. K, 7th Cav. Dec. 6, 1863 AL
YERKY, Robert G. B, 36th Cav. Bn. VA
YON, M. G. C, 25th Inf. Feb. 25, 1865 GA
YORK, Harrison F. H, 32nd Inf. Aug. 26, 1862 TN
YOST, Thomas. B, 18th Cav. Feb. 26, 1865 VA
YOUNG, Charles V. E, 47th Inf. Dec. 20, 1864 AL
YOUNG, Jarrett. I, 9th Cav. Jan. 31, 1865 TN
YOUNG, R. P. C, 32nd Inf. TN
YOUNG, T. B. C, 51st Inf. May 13, 1865 AL
YOUNG, William P. A, 32nd Inf. TN

Notes

Introduction

1. Bradley Omanson, "The Long March of John Wyeth," www.WorldWar1.com, February 2004.

Chapter 1

1. John A. Wyeth, "Cold Cheer at Camp Morton," *Century Monthly Magazine,* April 1891.
2. W. R. Holloway, "A Reply to 'Cold Cheer at Camp Morton,'" *Century Monthly Magazine,* September 1891.
3. J. K. Womack, "Treatment of Prisoners at Camp Morton," *Confederate Veteran,* December 1898.
4. Omanson.
5. John A. Wyeth, "Rejoinder to 'A Reply to "Cold Cheer at Camp Morton,"'" *Century Monthly Magazine,*September 1891.
6. Hattie Lou Winslow and Joseph R. H. Moore, *Camp Morton 1861-1865* (Indianapolis: Indiana Historical Society, 1940).
7. Ibid.

Chapter 2

1. Winslow and Moore.
2. Ibid.
3. Ibid.
4. Ibid.

5. Ibid.
6. Ibid.
7. Ibid.

Chapter 3

1. Winslow and Moore.
2. W. H. H. Terrell, *Indiana in the War of the Rebellion,* vol. 1 of *Report of the Adjutant General* (Indianapolis: 1869).
3. John K. Farris diaries, Special Collections Department, Robert W. Woodruff Library, Emory University.
4. Winslow and Moore.
5. Ibid.
6. Ibid.
7. Ibid.
8. Ibid.
9. Ibid.
10. John Martin Wood to his wife, from family collection.
11. Winslow and Moore.
12. Farris diaries.
13. Winslow and Moore.
14. Farris diaries.
15. Winslow and Moore.

Chapter 4

1. Patricia Faust, ed., *Historical Times Encyclopedia of the Civil War* (New York: Harper and Row, 1993).
2. Winslow and Moore.
3. Ibid.
4. Ibid.
5. Ibid.

Chapter 5

1. Faust.
2. Winslow and Moore.

3. National Park Service Southeast Archaeological Center Web site, "Andersonville Prison," www.cr.nps.gov, 2004.

4. Winslow and Moore.

5. Ibid.

6. Ibid.

7. Ibid.

8. Ibid.

9. "Treasonable Organizations: Sons of Liberty," www.countyhistory.com, 2004.

10. Winslow and Moore.

11. Ibid.

12. Ibid.

13. Ibid.

Chapter 6

1. Wyeth, "Cold Cheer."

2. Winslow and Moore.

3. Wyeth, "Cold Cheer."

4. Winslow and Moore.

5. Wyeth, "Cold Cheer."

6. Ibid.

7. Ibid.

8. Ibid.

9. Ibid.

10. Ibid.

11. Nathanial H. Ayres to his wife, from family collection.

Chapter 7

1. Winslow and Moore.

2. Holloway.

3. Ibid.

4. Ibid.

5. Ibid.

6. Wyeth, "Cold Cheer."

7. Holloway.

8. Ibid.

9. Ibid.
10. Ibid.
11. Ibid.

Chapter 8

1. Wyeth, "Rejoinder."
2. Editorial, *Buffalo Courier,* April 6, 1891.
3. Wyeth, "Rejoinder."
4. Ibid.
5. Ibid.
6. Ibid.
7. Ibid.
8. Ibid.
9. Ibid.
10. Ibid.
11. Ibid.
12. Ibid.
13. Ibid.

Chapter 9

1. Womack.
2. Ibid.
3. Ibid.
4. Ibid.
5. John Franklin Champenois, "Life in Camp Morton, 1863-1865," *Standard (Killen, Ala.),* 1912.
6. Ibid.
7. Ibid.
8. W. R. Houghton and M. B. Houghton, *Two Boys in the Civil War and After* (Montgomery, Ala.: Paragon, 1912).
9. Ibid.
10. Ibid.
11. Ibid.
12. Ibid.
13. Ibid.
14. Thomas E. Spotswood, "Horrors of Camp Morton," *Memphis*

Commercial, n.d. From "Southern Crossroads" Web site, www.csa-dixie.com.

15. Ibid.

16. J. G. Wilson, letter to the editor, *New York Times,* June 1867.

Chapter 10

1. *Indianapolis Journal,* June 14, 1865.

2. Winslow and Moore.

3. Henry Hays Forwood letters, Manuscripts Department, University of North Carolina—Chapel Hill.

4. Winslow and Moore.

5. Ibid.

Bibliography

Champenois, John Franklin. "Life in Camp Morton, 1863-1865." *Standard (Killen, Ala.)* (1912).

Confederate Burials in Crown Hill Cemetery, Marion County. Indianapolis: Crown Hill Cemetery.

Faust, Patricia, ed. *Historical Times Encyclopedia of the Civil War.* New York: Harper and Row, 1993.

Holloway, W. R. "A Reply to 'Cold Cheer at Camp Morton.'" *Century Monthly Magazine* (September 1891).

Houghton, W. R., and M. B. Houghton. *Two Boys in the Civil War and After.* Montgomery, Ala.: Paragon, 1912.

www.indianainthecivilwar.com.

National Park Service Southeast Archaeological Center Web site. "Andersonville Prison." www.cr.nps.gov (2004).

Omanson, Bradley. "The Long March of John Wyeth." www.WorldWar1.com (February 2004).

Spotswood, Thomas E. "Horrors of Camp Morton." *Memphis Commercial* (n.d.).

"Treasonable Organizations: Sons of Liberty." www.countyhistory.com (2004).

Winslow, Hattie Lou, and Joseph R. H. Moore. *Camp Morton 1861-1865.* Indianapolis: Indiana Historical Society, 1940.

Womack, J. K. "Treatment of Prisoners at Camp Morton." *Confederate Veteran* (December 1898).

Wyeth, John A. "Cold Cheer at Camp Morton." *Century Monthly Magazine* (April 1891).

———. "Rejoinder to 'A Reply to "Cold Cheer at Camp Morton."'" *Century Monthly Magazine* (September 1891).

Index

Alabama Hall of Fame, 99
Alton Prison, 92
American Medical Association, 22
Andersonville, 28, 50, 71
Arcemont, Goacin, 54
Ayres, Nathanial H., 62

Baron, C. S. S., 75
Battle of Corydon, 44
Battle of Perryville, Kentucky, 49
Ben-Hur, 18
Biddle, James, 43
Buffalo Courier, 74

Camp Chase, 93
Camp Douglas, 46, 92
Camp Morton controversy, 23-24
Camp Morton 1861-1865, 24, 44, 58
Century Monthly Magazine, 17-18, 20, 23, 25, 57, 65, 73, 83, 99
Champenois, John Franklin, 80
Clark, Augustus M., 47
"Cold Cheer at Camp Morton," 17-18, 23, 25, 57
Coleman, Christopher B., 24
Confederate Burials in Crown Hill Cemetery, Marion County, 97

Confederate Mound, 94, 97
Confederate Veteran, 20, 79, 97
Crown Hill Cemetery, 94-95
Cunningham, Sumner Achibald, 97

Department Encampment of the Grand Army of the Republic, 18, 65, 73, 79
Douglas, Stephen A., 30

1863 "Draft Riot," 50
Ekin, James A., 35
Elliott, William, 94
Elmira, 92

Farris, John K., 36, 39
Fifty-Third Alabama Cavalry, 86
Forrest, Nathan Bedford, 99
Fort Donelson, 36
Fort Sumter, 103
Forty-first Tennessee Volunteers, 36
Forwood, Henry Hays, 92
Foster, Thomas, 67
Fourth Alabama Cavalry, 17, 22

Gapen, P. M., 74

Garfield Park, 94
"Great Raid," 45
Greenlawn Cemetery, 93
Groves, W. H., 77

Halleck, Henry, 35
Hedges, Elijah, 67
Henderson, Samuel, 27, 33
Henderson's Grove, 97
Herron-Morton Place, 97, 101
Hervey, J. W., 67
Hobson, Edward, 45
Holloway, W. R., 18, 65, 99
Houghton, Mitchell B. and
    William Robert, 81

Indiana, 17, 22, 27, 30, 39, 44
Indiana Historical Society, 24
Indianapolis, 17, 22, 27-30, 35-
    36, 38, 44-45, 65, 93-94, 101
Indianapolis Journal, 91

Jacobs, Andy, 95

Kilgore, C. B., 23, 75
Kipp, Charles J., 67
Kitchen, John M., 67
Knights of the Golden Circle, 53

Lee, Robert E., 85
Libby Prison, 46
Lincoln, Abraham, 28, 30, 103
Louisville & Nashville Railroad,
    20

Memphis Commercial, 85
Mitchell, James L., 65
Moore, Joseph R. H., 24
Morgan, John Hunt, 20, 44-45
Morton, Oliver P., 18, 28, 38, 65

Nashville (Tenn.) Banner, 68
New York Daily News, 93
New York Polyclinic Medical
    School and Hospital, 22
New York Times, 88

oath of allegiance, 91
Owen, Richard, 35, 53, 98

parole system, 41
Parr, W. P., 20, 75
Pasco, S., 75

Quirk's Scouts, 20

Rainey, J. L., 76
"Rejoinder," 23
"Reply to 'Cold Cheer at Camp
    Morton, 'A,'" 20, 65
Rice, James H., 70
Rock Island Prison, 93
Rose, David Garland, 39

Sanger, E. L., 92
Second South Carolina Rifles, 62
Shelton, W. E., 76
Sherman, William T., 51
Sons of Liberty, 53-54
Spotswood, Alexander, 85
Spotswood, Thomas E., 85
States' Rights, 23
Stevens, Ambrose A., 49, 67, 98

Tenth Illinois Infantry, 22
Tucker, Samuel, 77
*Two Boys in the Civil War and
    After*, 81

Veteran Reserve Corps, 49, 67,
    91

Wallace, Lew, 18, 28, 65
War Department, 18
Wightman, W. S., 77
Wilcox, O. B., 70
Wilson, J. G., 88
Winder, Richard B., 51
Winder, W. Sidney, 50

Winslow, Hattie Lou, 24
Wirz, Henry, 28
Womack, J. K., 20, 79
Wood, John Martin, 38
Wyeth, John Allan, 17, 20, 57, 65, 73, 79, 99, 105